# Bio-Architecture

Javier Senosiain

AMSTERDAM  BOSTON
HEIDELBERG  LONDON
NEW YORK  OXFORD  PARIS
SAN DIEGO  SAN FRANCISCO
SINGAPORE  SYDNEY
TOKYO

Architectural Press
An imprint of Elsevier
Linacre House, Jordan Hill, Oxford OX2 8DP
200 Wheeler Road, Burlington, MA 01803

First published 2003

**British Library Cataloguing in Publication Data**
A catalogue record for this book is available from the British Library

**Library of Congress Cataloging in Publication Data**
A catalog record for this book is available from the Library of Congress

ISBN 0 7506 5604 2

Illustrations by Luis Raúl Enríquez Montiel
Translated by Marguerite Black Sterling

For information on all Architectural Press publications
visit our website at www.architecturalpress.com

Typeset by Genesis Typesetting Ltd, Rochester, Kent, UK
Printed and bound in Italy

# CONTENTS

Acknowledgements                                             vii

Prologue                                                    viii

Preface                                                       ix

**I   NATURE: OUR INSPIRATION                                 1**
Function in Nature                                             9
Space in Nature                                              15
Structure in Nature                                          25
Shape in Nature                                              45
The Snail                                                    47

**II  HUMANITY: OUR SPACE THROUGHOUT
      THE AGES                                               59**
Vernacular Architecture                                      60
Arches, Vaults, and Domes                                   77
The Modern City                                              89

**III THE ORGANIC: OUR NATURAL SPACE                        101**
Organic Architecture                                        102
The Search for Space                                        129
The Organic Habitat                                         137

Epilogue                                                    159

Figure Credits                                              161

References                                                  163

Selected Bibliography                                       167

Index                                                       171

# DEDICATION

With immense love and gratitude, I dedicate this book to my parents Juan and Blanca, as well as to my wife Paloma and my daughters Paloma and Natalia, who have accompanied me throughout this adventure.

# ACKNOWLEDGEMENTS

Many people have helped me, both in the idea for the book and in actually carrying out this idea. These include Daniel Arredondo, who showed sympathetic understanding about the considerable time I dedicated to this work whilst we were developing other projects; German Castro, who helped in the writing and revising of the text; and Luis Raúl Enríquez, who helped compile and produce the illustrations. The support these colleagues gave me was priceless and I cannot thank them enough.

I also wish to express my gratitude to León Faure, who began this book with me; to Norma Orduña, for stylistic revision; to Laura Garza, who allowed me access to her collection of books on mollusks, and to Marco Vilchis for his consistent support and interest in the written work. The construction of dwellings pictured towards the end of the book would never have been possible without the contributions of the 'maestro' Juan Sánchez and of those other people involved, all of whom I thank for their talent and dedication. Finally, I wish to thank Liz Whiting at Architectural Press for her tireless help and encouragement in moving this project forward, and for completing three of the sections for me.

# PROLOGUE

Sometimes architects also produce books. The material they use often reflects their own, or other people's, experiences in the exercise of their profession. The raw material used here, however, is broader: this book is full of biological analogies from every age.

Among the authors who, in recent decades, have been occupied with the analogical method of architectural creation are the outstanding George Collins and Geoffrey Broadbent. When discussing methods of design in architecture, the main question is whether or not there are procedures to which an architect can turn when he faces his main responsibility: to anticipate the shape that spaces will occupy. For Broadbent there is no doubt. The architect (or whoever assumes that role) can solve these problems in four ways: they can find the forms that geometry and its rules and precepts suggest (canonical method); arrive at conclusions after an arduous process of experimental trial and error, using the methods within their reach (pragmatic method); be inspired by other architectural forms or images already in existence (iconic method); or borrow forms which do not belong to the architectural world and convert them into shapes that are undoubtedly architectural (analogical method). The most frequent approach would be a combination of all of these.

Analogical work in architecture is full of references to form and biological function. Organic architecture appears under the headings of phytomorphic, zoomorphic or anthropomorphic, depending on the mythical and/or symbolic role that the producing culture assigns to plants, animals and humans. For that reason the meticulous research that Javier Senosiain has done on such biological analogies is stupendous. He has travelled far, not only in distance but also to times in which the relationships between humans and their natural surroundings were much closer than today. That is how the decorated Corinthian capital or the sanctuaries of Angkor, sculpted like gigantic human faces, should be seen; and that is how Senosiain shows them here.

But this study also returns to modern problems and even to local architectural culture. The different concepts that Frank Lloyd Wright or Frei Otto have of the organic, lead to new reflections of that term. The progress of scientific observation is related to biological analogies that surpass what is observable at first glance. For that reason Enrique Castañeda decades ago explored amoebic cellular forms, and that is why Agustín Hernández also arrived at solutions that adopted foetal forms for housing.

Javier Senosiain's own work outlined in the last part of this book is no less creative and, at the same time, owes much to this genealogy of architectural organic forms. I prefer to read the last chapter not as a conclusion but as the current limits of unfinished work. I think that its author still has many years ahead, and we can anticipate new contributions from him to this fascinating world of biological analogies in architecture.

*Alberto González Pozo*
*Architect and Theoretician*

# PREFACE

Harmony between man and his surroundings has, for me, always been the most profound motive for architectural tasks. This restless goal has taken me on a long search that finally crystallised in the concept of the Organic House.

Since his appearance on the earth, man has continuously transformed the environment for his own convenience, at an almost unlimited pace. This process has become faster in the last 50 years, especially in areas of civilisation and city planning. When man creates, he usually destroys the natural, forgetting that he and the rest of nature need to co-exist in harmony with each other.

Our technologically-advanced twentieth-century man feels great longing, nevertheless. This is what has generated this book. Organic Architecture is neither a recrimination of 'cultural evolution' nor a dark criticism of the errors that have been committed since architecture and city planning moved 'against nature'. Twenty years of investigation into the complex reticulate world of the organic are presented here with the passionate objective of a harmonious return to nature. It should not be misunderstood as an impossible return to the utopia of the 'happy savage'.

The first two chapters - covered by the term 'Nature-History' - reflect on the spaces which man can adapt; the last chapter shows how this can be done.

*Javier Senosiain*

'May this be, if not a voyage of discovery, at least an antidote to the bitter nostalgia often felt through our great losses and destructiveness... alea jacta est. '

# NATURE: OUR INSPIRATION

01

Love for Nature and sincerity. These are the two strong passions of genius. Everyone loves Nature... Have absolute faith in her. Be assured that she is never ugly, and limit your ambition to being loyal to her...

August Rodin, *Testament*, 1840–1917[1]

## Introduction

Nature itself is beautiful. In it we find an infinite variety of shapes, colours and species living together in a perfect, logical, unquestioning way. The only imperative for living in harmony with nature is mutual respect.

Early in their existence, humans stayed very close to nature. Their intimate and understanding relationship led to harmonious, or at least balanced, interaction. Time passed and they grew both in number and knowledge. Their attitudes changed to their surroundings, learning to protect themselves from inclement weather and enemies. Proud, blinded by feelings of superiority and power, they unwittingly became nature's enemy. As humans moved further and further away from their origins they constructed living spaces foreign to their earlier existence.

They turned away from nature and, at that moment, as architect González Gortázar points out, were expelled from Paradise.[2] They still feel a yearning for the nature they have deserted – they think of, remember, and even visit it recreationally! They go to parks, forests, mountains, lakes... and find this ancestral environment beautiful and authentic, while they perceive their own surroundings to be false and bankrupt.

Although humans frequently find themselves living in arid, inhospitable, hostile spaces, this is often all that city dwelling offers. Yet they want a world for their descendants in which humans are not impossibly distant from nature.

Evolution gradually proceeds through small genetically accepted changes. Natural wisdom is light years ahead of us in experience, systems and structures; three billion years of experience as compared to technology, still in its infancy, makes this inevitable. Even the humblest of nature's designs would offer us conditions more suitable to human satisfaction.[3] Ancient art was inspired by natural designs, although this tendency has gradually and little by little been lost. If we intend to rescue what has been lost, let us use the handbook that has not been, and never will be, out of date: *the Book of Nature*.

Jean-Jacques Rousseau, the French philosopher, commented that when our values are being destroyed, we tend to return to nature:[4] **'I do not fully know if man's values have been, or are in the process of being, destroyed, but why wait to find out?'**

Minimal effort exists to redirect human's views of nature, aiming to re-establish the equilibrium lost through rapid technological

**Figure 1.1**
Couple by lake. Humans still visit nature recreationally.

development. The ideal should be, in the near future, to reintegrate science, technology, and humanism, restoring a balanced relationship with nature and reducing the strains on natural resources. We already possess proof of the potential effectiveness of this in the Gaia approach.

The *Book of Nature* cannot be interpreted at first glance. Renowned architects, engineers and scientists are trying to decipher its messages, analysing wide ranges of natural phenomena such as the structures of the throats of lizards or frogs, the framework of spiders' webs, a bird's flight, how insects function, or the 'design' and form of a fish's behaviour in water. They observe the principles of the animal, vegetable and mineral kingdoms in order to apply them to human life and so improve it.

Some aspects of nature are undetectable to the human eye, but have been discovered by science. It has been established, for example, that bats can fly in an oriented and precise fashion without optical vision because they have their own radar.

Studies of this type are being carried out within the very young science of Bionics in order to apply them as Human needs. The word 'Bionics' derives from the Greek *bios* (life) and *ikos* (unit): a living unit, a term that refers to all artificial constructions modelled after living systems. Jack E. Steele of the US Air Force used the word with this meaning for the first time in 1960 at a meeting at the Wright-Patterson Air Force Base in Dayton, Ohio.

Bionics is interested in the creation of functions and forms analogous to those of the living organism. This is achieved by means of observation and thorough research, analysis and synthesis. This science does not attempt to trace or copy; it works on the thesis that every model can potentially provide ideas for the design of new methods and mechanics that will improve those currently existing.

To reach its objectives, bionics links different sciences such as psychology, electronics, maritime engineering and aeronautics, among others. These interdisciplinary developments have reached important goals, always based on designs provided by nature. Take, for example, the parallels between a computer and the nervous or cerebral system of a human, or even the radar used in marine navigation and that of the dolphin. Background and wider reading is attractively presented in Stewart's (1998) book entitled *Life's Other Secret*.[5]

Bionics can be used for our principle goal: the achievement of a better habitat for humans. We analyse nature and apply its principles to the design of our spaces. An example of this is the new urban design by Paolo Soleri which he called Archology (architecture + ecology = Archology), inspired by the way that the cells of an organism are distributed. See chapters in Borden and Dunster (1995; 1996) for further reading.[6]

An architect's aim in design is to shape things in such a way that they fulfil their functions perfectly. Bionics studies not only the physical and chemical aspects of a natural model, but also the morphology of its structures, in order to apply them to the construction of artificial devices and systems that will later be used by people.

An ever-changing evolutionary process is maintained in nature so that inefficient systems disappear, while those characteristics that are better able to adapt to prevalent, or developing, environmental conditions, can be perfected. When inspired by these models, we can take advantage of this process of improvement and adapt it to our designs.

Throughout history, nature has inspired humans to progress in science and technology. In the year 400 BC, Democritus, a philosopher from ancient Greece, said: **'We learn important things from imitating animals. We are apprentices of the spider, imitating her in the task of weaving and confecting clothing. We learn from the swallows how to construct homes, and we learn to sing from both the lark and the swan...'**[7]

Bionics is applicable to the designs of different branches of science, in land, sea, and air transportation, and elsewhere.

The first cars that used an internal combustion engine looked like simple boxes on wheels. They followed the design of a stagecoach pulled by horses, but used a motor instead of the horses. Designers had not yet considered the resistance of air imposed on an accelerating vehicle.

In 1933, Buckminster Fuller designed a car based on a natural shape. By studying the shape of the raindrop, Fuller designed the Dymaxion automobile based on the same principles. He knew that air resistance increased in ratio to velocity squared. For example: if the car tripled its speed, air resistance would be nine times greater; the faster it went, the more the strength of the motor would be reduced as it pushed air to the sides.

Fuller deduced that the shape of the car was inefficient and should be modified. He found the solution when he studied the few notes that had been written on the properties of aerodynamics which showed that when a drop of rain falls through the atmosphere, its spherical shape is modified: the front part of a raindrop remains rounded and supports most of the fluid, while the back, lateral edge, is shaped by air currents. In this way, the friction of a raindrop against the air gives it the shape of a tear.

By changing the shape of the ordinary car, there were also other advantages. Fuller's car, using a standard V-8 purchased from the Ford factory, easily reached speeds of up to 190 kilometres per hour. A motor with three times the power would have been necessary to accomplish the same feat, using any existing design. This is one of the few examples in which we observe function following shape.

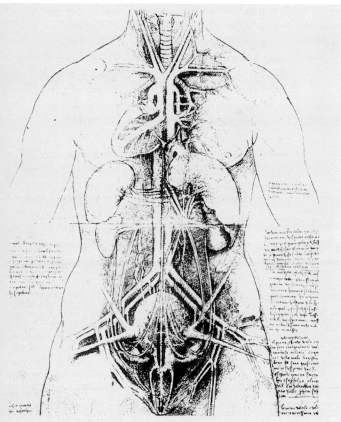

**Figure 1.2**
The anatomical sketch by Leonardo da Vinci.

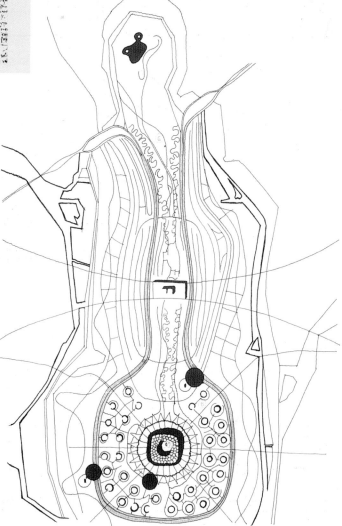

**Figure 1.3**
Analogy of Mesa City conceived organically by Paolo Soleri.

Similarly, the development of aeronautical engineering derives, to a great degree, from the observation of flying creatures. The first flying machines were inspired by the flight of butterflies and bats, winged creatures that are light in weight and have wide surfaces used for gravity compensation. The challenge that faced the human race was to keep themselves airborne...

Leonardo da Vinci is the best-known example of an inventor who designed plans for a flying machine which imitated a bat. A bat's membranous, impermeable skin covers and reinforces the skeleton of the wings and undoubtedly this principle was vital to his design.

Four hundred years later the bat also inspired the first machine able to fly: Ader's device. After carefully measuring the skeleton of a bat, Ader built a similar frame on an enlarged scale using interwoven bamboo poles. He then covered this 'skeleton' with silk cloth in lieu of the bat's skin.

As time went by, people wanted to increase the speed of their flying machines with more powerful compact motors; they therefore observed birds, their flight conditions and how they overcame air resistance. Designers applied the results of these observations to airships, and they are still very similar in aerodynamic design to birds to this day.

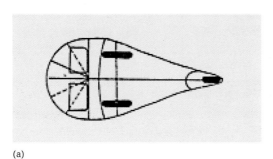

(a)

**Figure 1.4**

The Dymaxion car designed in 1933 by Fuller; (b) prototype designed by General Motors for the twenty-first century; (c) effects of wind: Dymaxion and conventional automobile.

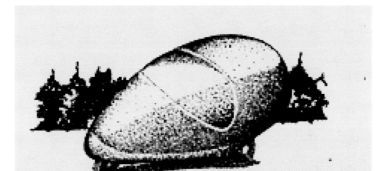

(b)

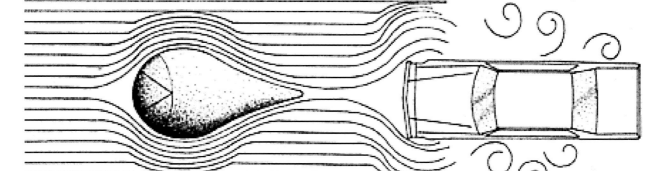

(c)

**Figure 1.5**
(a) Flying machine and bat wings; (b) skate and Horton twin-jet fighter bomber; (c) shark and F-101A jet; (d) killer whale and jumbo jet.

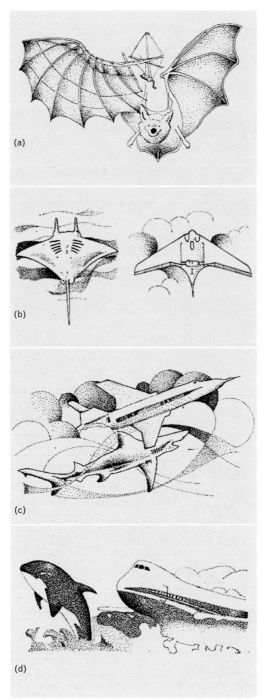

The beak of a bird and the nose of an aeroplane both cut the air in front, making displacement faster and lighter. The cabin – the pilot's viewpoint – is comparable to the eyes of the bird. The wings of both bird and aeroplane, with ailerons and flaps, help achieve fluidity, execute manoeuvres in the air, and permit landing. The tails of both are used to direct, and give momentum to, flight. The position of the landing gear is similar to that of the bird's feet.

In an effort to fly at even greater speeds and conquer space, we were later inspired by aquatic animals. Water is more resistant to movement than air and the idea of jet stream propulsion was conceived. Different aspects of the shark, manta ray, whale, squid, and so on, were applied to the design of spaceships, since the hydrodynamic shapes of these animals facilitate displacement in water. The skate, capable of instant mobility at surprising speed due to the principle of water displacement, served as a physical and analogical model for the construction of pursuit planes. The manta ray is impelled through the water by a propeller and that provided the inspiration for jet turbines, devices absorbing air in the same way as the skate takes in water through the mouth and ejects it through the gills. The same analogical principle was used in the F-101A jet in 1954: the shark provided the basis for its design.

The shape of a dolphin's nose applied in the prow area of boats is an excellent application of bionics in the design of aquatic transportation. Skin-diving equipment, such as fins, has been designed from the shapes of marine animals.

**Figure 1.6**
Model of Frog
Motorcycle. Luigi
Colani.

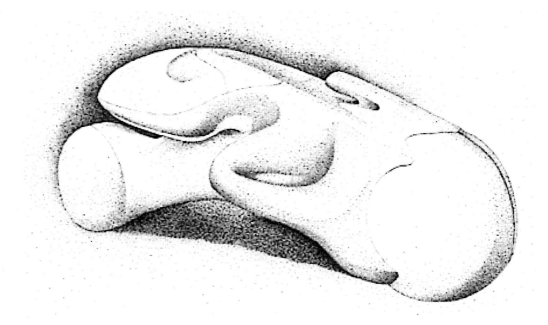

Designs for the creation of useful objects have been based on the human body itself. For example, primitive people used to drink water from cupped hands and this inspired the shape for bowls and plates. Industrial design took the joints of the elbow, arm and hand as a model for the backhoe. In Gothic architecture, the arm and hand were used as basic principles for the design of the enormous columns that support buildings: the column represents the arm and the branchings that reduce the stress on the vault represent fingers.

**Figure 1.7**
Strand of hair stalk
and chimney.

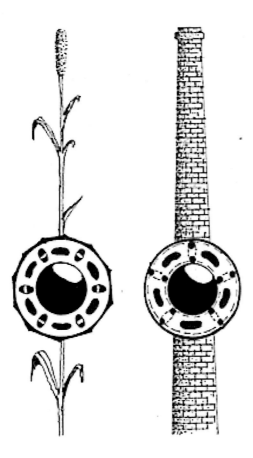

In this way, designers, through intelligence and intuition, often come to conclusions, the principles of which relate to those in nature, even when not acquainted with them. Examples include the similarities between a tall factory chimney and a human hair: both structures are hollow, and the tissues are peripheral. What could be thought to be coincidence isn't really. When we consider height – in the one, to dispose of toxic gases, and in the other to capture solar rays – the chimney and the human hair are influenced by the same physical conditions: mechanical forces, resistance to wind, proportion between height and base, and so on. Similar problems often produce similar solutions.

As we can see, the organic systems of natural structures – from microscopic protozoans or diatoms to large mammals – harmoniously express mathematical relationships and embrace beauty, function, simplicity and economy. All of these are ideals in design and have therefore inspired us. The designs of the German engineer, architect and sculptor Luigi Colani are examples. Using modern materials and technology, he shows us the face of the twenty-first century.

Below are some primary examples of the innumerable applications of bionics.

# NATURE DESIGN

| | |
|---|---|
| Sail fish | Sailing boat |
| Hatchet fish | Hatchet |
| Swordfish | Sword |
| Hammerhead | Hammer |
| Sawfish | Saw |
| Dolphin | Torpedo |
| Dragonfly | Helicopter |
| Retina of the eye | Photographic camera |
| Bat | Radar |
| Front claws of a crab | Tweezers, pliers |
| Nautilus | Submarine |
| Nervous system | Computer |
| Fish scales | Tiles, shingles |
| Feet of aquatic birds | Swimming fins |
| Dorsal fins of fish | Keel of boats |
| Cobwebs | Nets |
| Oyster | Hinge |
| Root | Foundation |
| Eggshell | Dome |
| Animal mimicry (mimesis) | Camouflage |
| Eyelashes | Visor |
| Octopus suckers | Rubber cupping devices |
| Turtle shells | Armour |
| Caterpillar | Tank |
| Nipple | Pacifier |
| Insect antennae | Television antennae |
| Anthill | City |
| Anteater | Vacuum cleaner |
| Flying squirrel | Glider |
| Parakeet | Wrench |
| Bird feather | Fountain pen |
| Tree trunk, arm | Column |
| Ear | Radar |

# Function in nature

One of the essential aspects of both natural and manmade design is functionalism.

Function is intimately related to form; there is no form without function, or function without form. Neither can exist without the other.

In 1896, Sullivan declared that: '**shape comes after function.**'[8] Le Corbusier wrote that as far as he was concerned, '**Plants grow from the inside out, the exterior part being the result of the interior.**'[9] However, on rare occasions, form can also determine function. In any case, form–function or function–form is an unreal dilemma. Once an artisan becomes fully acquainted with the materials they don't debate whether form or function is the more important – they're interrelated. Nowadays we often complicate that simplicity.

In nature, things are functional in relation to the whole. The purpose of legs, for instance, is to support and move the body, yet on their own they are unstable.

If we study the shape and characteristics of many things in nature, we find that they have precise reasons for being as they are; their shapes fulfil functions, and they are therefore always beautiful. The nostrils of a human nose open downwards to prevent rain and perspiration entering. They are also located high enough to reduce the entrance of dust that floats near or at ground level. Hairs inside the nostrils serve to filter inhaled air.

Function, as an autonomous architectural concept, has a physical and psychological aspect. Physical, material or physiological functions are comprised of concepts such as economy, time, movement and position. Psychological function is

❝Nature is a self-made machine, more perfectly automated than any automated machine. To create something in the image of nature is to create a machine, and it was by learning the inner workings of nature that man became a builder of machines ❞

Eric Hoffer

At the time Mathias Goeritz, creator of the Museo Eco, was writing his *Manifiesto de la Arquitectura Emocional (Manifesto of Emotional Architecture)* in which he said that architecture needed a more spiritual element in order to rescue itself from the purely material function into which it was falling.

Creation is a long, difficult road that requires logical and orderly, as well as creative, imagination. Taking into account the maxim of Ortega y Gasset that: **'the mission of art is to invent what does not exist'**,[11] it becomes almost impossible to establish a method by which we can practise architecture.

**Figure 1.8**
Chapel at the convent of the Madres Capuchinas, Luis Barragán, 1952–1956.

comprised of such concepts as joy, serenity and tranquillity (i.e. stability and achievement).

Richard Neutra explained their importance with the following anecdote. He received a phone call in the middle of the night from a woman whose house he had planned and built. She complained that there was a leak, and the water dripping into her bedroom was keeping her from sleeping. He realised there was a small problem with a technical aspect (material function) in her home. However, this small problem had made her very upset because it affected the psychological function: she needed a comfortable home where she and her family would feel happy.

Which is the more important, material or psychological function? The psychological function is fundamentally important to whoever lives in that space. Nevertheless, both are necessary for they each complement the other and together fulfil just one function.

The architect, Luis Barragán, was once asked what the difference was between his structures and those built by most other architects. He replied that while both took the material function into consideration, he considered other factors to be equally important – factors that would create a mood in the inhabitant such as emotion, serenity, or surprise.

When functional architecture was at its height in Mexico, an experimental museum was created, El Museo Eco, which generated controversy in different parts of the world. Michael Seuphor described it as: **'A group of asymmetrical arrangements organised in successive surprises, by means of corridors, walls, openings, and closed-up spaces, a sort of artistic poem through which one may walk**.'[10]

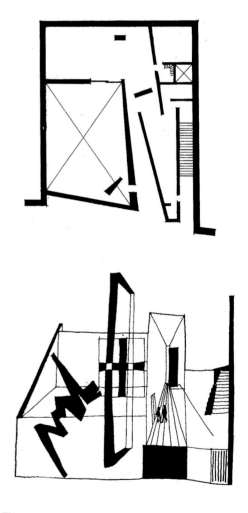

**Figure 1.9**
Diagram of the Museo Eco by Mathias Goeritz.

**Figure 1.10**
Diagramme of the
function of a house.

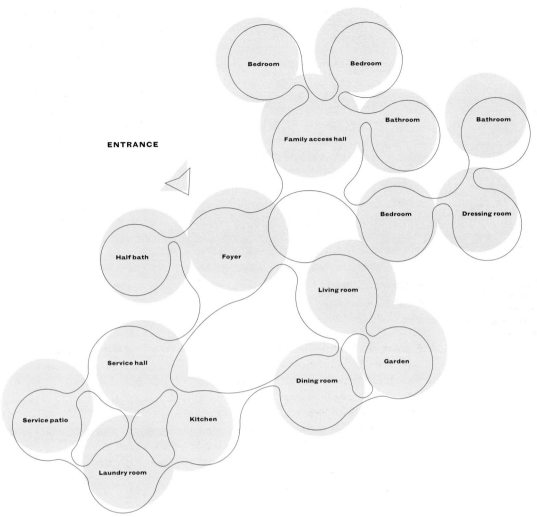

Nevertheless, there are ways of approaching the problem that help us to get closer to it. In most cases it is worth following some kind of design procedure as order encourages creative freedom. Function is important; it is an integral part of the creative process of design.

The first step, INFORMATION, consists of listing both physical and psychological requirements, taking into account the cultural and contextual conditions of the project; these two characterise organic architecture. The second step is based on INVESTIGATION, which is the search for, and analysis of, similar projects. The third step is FUNCTION, which can be defined as an 'organogram', a sort of diagram which shows the link that exists between one organ and another; the likeness to this or that organ or cell is called a zone or space (see Figure 1.10).

An embryonic whole (organs with correct location and proportion) must be envisaged in order to continue the gestation process until reaching SYNTHESIS, which will require a corresponding conceptual image. The importance of CONCEPT is especially stressed in the CREATIVE PROCESS described in Figure 1.11.

In order to arrive at a good conceptual image, a designer must be, as Rodin said:'**a free and spontaneous creator: he should not submit himself to a preconceived set of norms, and he should mistrust whatever could sterilise inspiration.**'[12]

To achieve originality, freedom, and spontaneity, any red tape must be put aside. Creativity is hard work: it requires brain cells and sensitivity. In other words, to quote Felix Candela: '**We should exert all our efforts, all**

| Information | | Investigation | Function | Synthesis |
|---|---|---|---|---|

**Figure 1.11**
Creative process

our capacity for distressed and anxious work, in the elaboration of any task we decide to start. In order for the final result to be considered a work of art, however, it must seem to have been accomplished without any effort, as if it were the fruit of playful and careless inspiration.'[13]

A successful result requires clear knowledge and consideration of all the following: the programme of needs; environmental factors such as dominant winds, topography and orientation; cultural, political and economic conditions; and functions including area analysis and zoning. When all this information is gathered together, it is then sifted to remove anything superfluous and abstract, leaving only what is essential. This is then compacted, and synthesis is made possible. Finally a time of 'torment and pain' arrives before attaining fully that wonderous moment, so impossible to describe: the moment of inspiration, the germination of an idea, the birth of a concept.

Later the concept is expressed and adapted in the PRELIMINARY DESIGN, then polished in the EXECUTIVE DESIGN in an effort to attain a harmonious whole: unity.

The first stages of the creative process (Information, Investigation and Functional Scheme) must clearly and firmly lay the foundations on which the design will be established. If the placement of a zone or space in these first steps is incorrect, the design will be difficult to correct. It is vitally important to observe and analyse the process from the very beginning.

To arrive at an effective conceptual image, it is not enough to have a brilliant vision. As Ronald Conrad affirms: '**The creative act in general will be the result of continued and vigorous labour, the fruit of many years of constant dedication and mental effort... I am afraid that this is the only way to acquire the constructive inspiration yearned for so ardently by young architects and students....**'[14] And that is true: 99 per cent of the brilliance of genius is the result of one's own hard work and the remaining 1 per cent is inspiration. Inspiration reveals work that is conceived in the

**Figure 1.12**
Arriving at a successful result is like placing the fruits of research into a funnel, mixing and sifting the elements to synthesise an end-product.

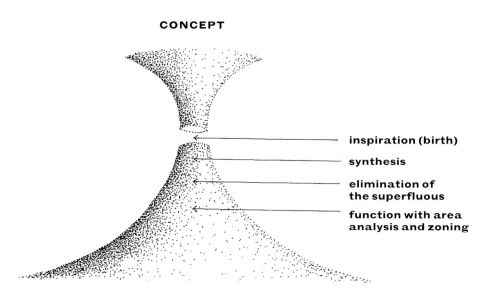

**CONCEPT**

inspiration (birth)
synthesis
elimination of the superfluous
function with area analysis and zoning

**GESTATION**
cultural determinants | program of necessities | ambient condition determinants

# Architecture must be universal yet still maintain the stamp of the people who produced it and of the place where it originated

CONTEXT
Adaptation to the topography.
Utilisation of existing material.

IDENTITY
Cultural roots:
Quetzalcoatl – plumed serpent.
God of wisdom.

(a)

(b)

(c)

(d)

(e)

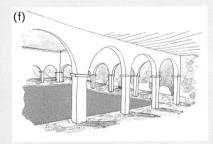
(f)

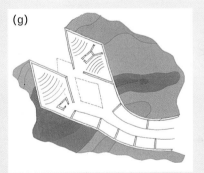
(g)

## CONCEPTUAL IMAGE

This preliminary design for twelve interdisciplinary institutes was developed on a piece of land made up of volcanic rock near the Cuicuilco circular pyramid in University City (the National University in Mexico City). Access to each institute is by way of the ring road, and the parking lots are located beside each institute according to the topography of the place. The libraries, which contain so many heavy books, are located on the ground floor as that is the largest area. The administrative offices are on the first floor, with the research cubicles on the second. A terraced roof makes it possible to move from one institute to another, or enter the auditoria and the cafeteria in the serpent's head. Co-ordination of all the institutes is found in the tail, coiled like the Cuicuilco pyramid.

**Figure 1.13**
(Parts a–g) City in the Investigation of the Humanities, Ciudad Universitaria, Mexico City, Mexico. Luis Enríquez and Javier Senosiain, 1987.

**Figure 1.14**
Graphic scheme of the creative process. Within the creative process, sequence and constancy are determining factors in achieving good design.

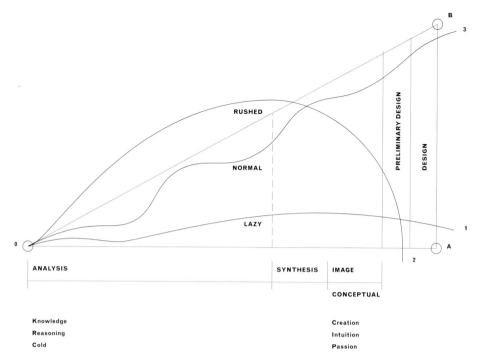

subconscious. If the mind is consistently occupied in a disciplined way with a certain problem, it can 'suddenly' find an appropriate solution.

Of course, inspiration and imagination are often related. Einstein believed that imagination is more important than knowledge because he considered knowledge limited whilst imagination is not. On the contrary, imagination stimulates progress because it permits evolutionary leaps.

In classical Greek, the word for 'to light' (one's way) is the same as the word for 'idea' or 'inspiration.' A problem seen in a new light becomes clear. Generally this 'new light' is personal; as the American novelist Truman Capote said: '...in the end, your style is you.'

Jean Cocteau said: **'Imagination does not come while you rock in a hammock waiting for it....'**[15] Rather, it is a sudden, immediate and total vision of a solution that you know is right. Frank Lloyd Wright gave his followers these instructions: **'If you want to design well, do not sit down at your drawing board with pencil, ruler, and triangle in hand... I have the whole idea in my mind... I could alter it substantially but the whole time that I have it, it is germinating.'**[16] Before sitting down to draw, the idea must already be clearly conceived.

It is possible that for some this approach will be too abstract. Nevertheless, in his *Architectural Programs and Manifestos of the Twentieth Century*, Hermann Muthessius speaks of the spontaneous and creative artist:[17]

*'The artist in himself is by essence a fervent individualist, a free and spontaneous creator; he never submits himself to a discipline that imposes a type or a set of rules on him..., he withdraws from all those who preach a norm or who could prevent him from following his train of thought, his own ideas that lead to his own, free goal, or that want to enclose him in some mold...'*

Art is a proof of liberty. The person who succeeds in the creative process seeks and finds, thinks, brainstorms and accomplishes. August Rodin mentioned this in his will: **'Do not waste your time in renewing mundane or political relationships... Love your mission passionately. There is none other as beautiful. It is much more lofty than is commonly believed... The world will only be happy when all men have an artist's soul, that is when everyone feels the pleasure of his labour....'**[18]

The true artist, therefore, expresses what he or she thinks, even at the risk of contradicting all established views, in that way teaching frankness to others. Rodin ends: **'Let us imagine the wonderful progress that would be achieved if suddenly absolute truth reigned among men! How soon society would let go of her errors and of her frankly confessed ugliness, and with what rapidity the earth would be converted into a paradise!'**[19]

## Space in nature

❝And swept away by an ardent desire, and impatient to see the large number of diverse and rare shapes created by the skill of nature, I spent a good while moving about among the shadowy rocks until I found myself at the mouth of a great cavern before which I stayed, a little confused as I did not know what it was all about, and there I remained with the waist arched, my left hand resting on my knee, and my right hand serving as a screen against my wrinkled brow. I turned about several times from one side to the other to see if I could catch a glimpse of something but was unable to do so due to the great darkness in the cavern. I remained there for some time until two feelings suddenly rose up from within: fear and desire. Fear of the threatening, dark cavern and the desire to see if there might be something marvellous inside it ❞

Leonardo da Vinci[20]

### The Womb

The first experience any human being has of space is the mother's womb. Bachelard described it as the: **'closed, protected, limited confines that care for the development of the being, of that being which emerges from a reduced space on the inside, so deep inside that it is formed from the inside out.'**[21]

A mother's womb is the optimum environment for development; there the foetus, surrounded by lukewarm amniotic fluid, enjoys equable temperature and balanced nutrition in an environment that absorbs any possible physical trauma that light or impact could normally produce. It is lulled by body movement and the rhythm of the mother's heartbeat. It would be hard indeed to find a better initial space in the world.

The loss of that space at the moment of birth is shocking. The baby is confronted by new space – an offensive, alien environment filled with bright lights, odours, voices and clatter.

Within a few moments of birth, he or she is exposed to medicines, a rigid feeding schedule and harsh changes in temperature, until reaching the arms of mother. She rocks her baby rhythmically, creating a moving cradle reminiscent of the womb and protecting it from adverse physical and psychological elements. The mother wraps the baby in different ways, recreating the movement, position and space that he or she will unconsciously recall throughout its life.

Child, adolescent and adult all seek similar atmospheres, places or feelings that will remind them of their first home. Sleeping positions often imitate a baby's position in the womb. Similarly, children's activities imitate movement in the womb: swinging on the swings, rocking, sliding down spiral-shaped slides, spinning around on merry-go-rounds. Sports with movement continue to be favourites. In the words of Levy Bruhl: **'In every primitive spirit, whatever his intellectual development may be, exists something fundamental that cannot be eradicated from his primitive mentality.'**[22]

**Figure 1.15**
An Indian mother: her shawl protects her child physically and psychologically. © Alejandro Martinez Mena.

**Figure 1.16**
A cave – natural architecture, magical and mysterious.

### The Cave

Bachelard stated that at the present time: **'before being thrown out into the world, man is deposited in the cradle of the house and afterwards the house becomes a huge cradle.'**[23] Long before Humans invented the cradle or began to build houses, Nature offered them generous caves giving the shelter and protection they instinctively sought.

Humans have always needed a covered refuge on their own scale. Although we appreciate the horizon, open spaces, great valleys or plains, and find joy in them as landscapes, we always want a place that will protect us. Caves were our first shelter from inclement weather, savage beasts, and enemies of our own species. This was the origin of architecture: architecture is nothing more than the control of adverse natural forces for the benefit of one's own well-being.

A cave, as natural architecture, arises from erosion of the earth, and its characteristics are found in noteworthy contributions to architecture. Gustavino the Elder gave his impression upon finding a cave and his awe of the 'constructive designs' that the cave suggested to him: **'...all this colossal space has been covered by only one piece... without frame or scaffold..., without heavy beams..., all made of particles placed one on top of another just as nature put them there. From that moment, I have been convinced that we have much to learn from that great book called Nature.'**[24]

Thinking about the caves of Gustavino the Elder and Leonardo da Vinci is exciting, but they also make us reflect on the architecture that humans build. Most caves are protective, warm, and extremely solid, but they're rarely on sale or for rent. Bernard Rudofsky had this to say: **'...until now real estate agents have continued to offer us fragile homes, toys for strong winds and floods, that constitute no refuge against the fury of nature. Compared to the cavern, the modern house is as unprotected as a birdcage.'**[25]

Frank Lloyd Wright, following this train of thought, said that a house should be like a cave, a refuge to which man could retire to protect himself against rain, wind and light. **'There he should be unrestricted, in complete security and rest, like an animal in its den.'**[26]

### Territory

Many studies exist on the behaviour of animals and their ability to adapt and develop. Zoologists

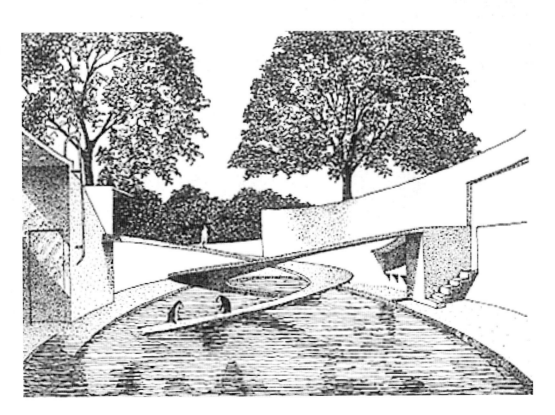

**Figure 1.17**
Habitat for penguins in the London Zoo: Lubetkin, Drake and Tecton, 1933.

and ecologists study animals in the wild for educational, cultural, and even commercial purposes. Lots of data has been collected relating to the type and dimensions of space each animal requires, and the precise environmental conditions needed for survival and reproduction in captivity. The results of this research are put into practice to reproduce their habitats as closely as possible.

Unfortunately such data has not yet been properly applied to the construction of a human's habitat, in spite of advances in sciences such as anthropology, psychology, and sociology, in human development, in the way of life, and how we live in our environment.

For many reasons living organisms tend to delimit their space. This extent of land is their 'territory' and it may be fixed by an individual, couple, sect or group, or even by a nation or species.

In the animal kingdom territory is fixed and marked in an apparently informal but deliberate way; this selectivity fulfils specific purposes. There are birds that mark their territory with songs and trills during the mating season, keeping strangers at a distance. Bears do the same, but by scratching and tearing at the bark of surrounding trees. Stags use a penetrating odour that comes from a gland close to their nostrils, while wolves urinate around the boundary of their territory.

In animals, territory is determined by physical needs, which include reproduction, food, security and shelter. Territories expand as food grows scarce, but decrease as food abounds. Animals frequently seek small territories that are easier to defend and protect.

Humans also define territories, but for political, cultural, economic, social and psychological reasons, as well as physical ones. They need to identify their property and possessions throughout life; they speak of their bedroom, their house, their neighbourhood, their city, their country, and so on.

They also make spaces for themselves that do not necessarily imply ownership but which are used for personal development. For example, a student will choose a seat at the far end of the library facing the wall to avoid distractions, whereas in a restaurant that same person will choose a seat in the corner but facing outwards, so as to feel relaxed and secure, among other reasons.

An example of space management in psychological terms is the way that Adolph Hitler used space in his office. A visitor who entered by the large door saw the desk of the Führer at the far end. As the visitor came further and further into this monumental space, he felt smaller and smaller so that when he finally reached the desk, he felt truly insignificant, weak, and vulnerable. It is clear that humans delimit territories in accordance with needs and possibilities.

Centuries before housing was constructed, animals built dwellings with great ability, using materials from both the vegetable and mineral kingdoms. These shelters were, and still are, varied and in every case these are authentic examples that should be followed. Examples of animal dwellings in aerial, terrestrial, amphibious and aquatic species are discussed below.

**Figure 1.18**
Open space, semi-open space, covered space.

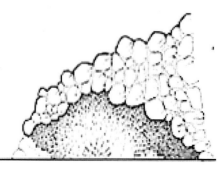

## Air Space: Nests

When spring comes to the northern hemisphere, a large variety of birds emigrate south in search of a climate warm enough to ensure reproduction. With their surprisingly muscular bodies, strong hearts, good digestion and energetic metabolisms, birds are tireless builders. They generally choose to build their nests in trees, on separate branches. The nests provide temporary homes for each couple and the offspring that they will sooner or later produce. They will announce, from the top of a tree or fence, that this is their territory and that none should trespass, and they protect this territory passionately.

Once a site has been chosen, both female and male sing while they build the nest. The male flies off to gather more materials while the female sculpts the nest with her beak, moulding it into the shape of her breast. After mating, the female lays her eggs in the nest and incubates them until the young, growing inside the eggs, break the shells with their beaks. During this simple process, the young birds are born and make themselves comfortable in the nest.

Twigs (or moss) and mud (or droppings) are the raw materials used to build the nest; the twigs work in favour of tension, while the mud ensures compression. The principles of tension and compression have been applied in this type of nest for more than 150 million years.

Reinforced concrete, following the same principle, has been used in construction for only a few years; it was not until near the end of the twentieth century that metallic fibre, fibreglass and other fibres were added to concrete to reinforce it further. Plastic resins reinforced with fibreglass follow the same idea.

Some birds live in hollows inside tree trunks or cavities in the earth. Those that can't find suitable hollows in trees make one. Such a bird is the woodpecker, which uses its beak as a tool. The following evolutionary span outlines the building of nests according to the characteristics of particular species.

There are currently some 9000 bird species and so a great diversity of nest types exists. All follow similar principles of location and adaptation; all take into account predominating winds, sunlight, humidity, size of eggs and parents, type of protection needed, and so on, but all are adapted to the needs of the constructing species.

Some nests are surprising constructions, like the so-called condominium nests. They are occupied by numerous couples or females and built as a single structure, but with separate spaces for each member. By integrating in this way, they have greater protection against predators.

**Figure 1.19**
(a) Nest of the weaver-bird; (b) vertical nest; (c) an ovenbird's nest; (d) tailor-bird's nest; (e) a floating nest; (f) bird colony.

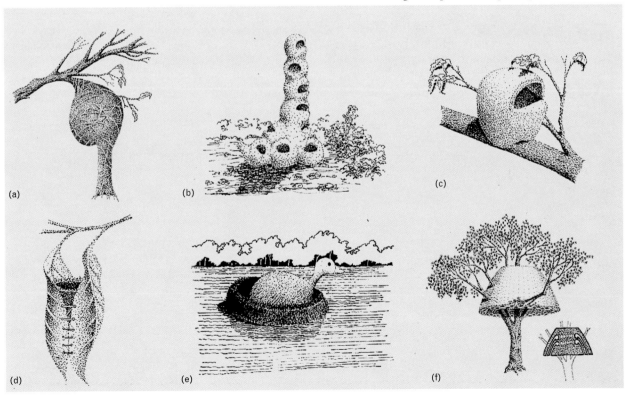

(a)     (b)     (c)

(d)     (e)     (f)

'Hanging' nests, made by weaver birds in tropical or very hot regions, are built so that they are practically hanging from the tree. The entrance, at the bottom of a sort of tunnel, prevents possible attacks from snakes or other animals, and also protects the birds from sunlight and rain.

'Vertical' nests made with mud and straw, are similar to apartment houses. Each opening is a complete, individual nest containing two chambers, the first is a 'hall', the second is for sleeping in and for laying and incubating eggs. The mass of earth stabilises the inside temperature.

Ovenbirds (so-called because of the shape of their nests) build nests of clay mixed with horsehair or very thin, fibrous roots, to make the structure more solid and to avoid cracks. They pick up the horsehair (or roots) and roll it in mud until it becomes a small ball the size of a hazelnut; this is then taken to the nest site. The nest is moulded from the inside with a deep, wide opening like a baker's oven. A human hand could easily reach inside the first compartment but not the second, which is therefore built as protection. The second compartment, barely 30 centimetres across, is semi-spherical and can be completely closed. The inside, where the eggs are laid, is lined with soft, dry grass. This nest is so resistant that it can survive undamaged for years.

The tailor-bird builds its nest with great dexterity: taking two palm leaves, it uses its beak to perforate their edges and then sew them together with plant fibres, strands of cotton, or spider webs, finishing off with a knot. This finally forms the required bag.

Troglodyte nests are found inserted into steep, sandy hillsides or cliffs. The birds dig small caves and protect the entrance with a hanging plant acting as a curtain.

Marine swallows build floating nests. Similar to a raft made of plants and herbs, they are anchored to the root of an old tree or branch so that they rise and fall with the water. The same technique is used in the construction of floating homes such as those in Hong Kong and Sausalito, California.

As part of the mating ritual, the male bowerbird of New Guinea and Australia decorates its nest with moss, orchids, feathers, seeds and shells. He paints these as a bower using his beak as paintbrush dipped in vegetable pigments or fruit pulp and creating an elaborate decorative collage.

## Land Space: the Termite Nest

Amazing terrestrial constructions exist in the animal kingdom as well. The termite nest in particular is a monumental achievement. These insects, 'white ants', generally live in the tropics. They can only live in hot climates, but their skins do not protect them from the sun. Their bodies are soft, they are usually blind, and they need constant levels of humidity and temperature.

Termites have, however, a sophisticated social system which makes urbanised development possible. Directed by the queen, the workers build massive constructions in accordance with their needs.

Termites adopt an infinite number of nest forms but they all use similar materials and ways of controlling temperature. The structures vary according to climate: tropical species build enormous masses around 5 to 8 metres high, so large and numerous as to look like a town made up of huts; in Africa the nests are similar to giant mushrooms; elsewhere, they resemble castles with towers or campaniles.

One of the most extraordinary structures is the Compass Knoll made by Australian termites. This is some 3 metres long, nearly 4 metres high, and a little more than 1 metre wide. It is built transversally from east to west and longitudinally from north to south. The orientation can be explained by the need for protection from the sun's strong rays. The towers that these insects construct can reach a height of up to eight hundred times their own size. By comparison, the Petronas Twin Towers in Kuala Lumpur are just over two hundred times the height of an average person.

The size of their constructions is admirable but so too is their building method and design. Termites use the body as a tool: the upper jaw serves as a spoon, the antennae as a basis for measurement. The basic material used is dirt that they make more solid by using saliva or gastric juices as mortar. Other termites combine dirt with particles of digested wood, and often with the products of other insects with which they have an agreement. Whichever technique is used, their nests are impressively hard and durable. A termite knoll found in road construction near what is now Harare, Zimbabwe, was found to be 700 years old and was only destroyed by using dynamite. Glue companies often study the reactions of chemicals in termite saliva and gastric juices in order to develop their adhesives.

A single termite knoll can easily accommodate three million insects, all directed by a queen from the royal chamber located in the middle of the nest. Galleries with halls branch out

**Figure 1.21**
Termite hill in Kenya, Africa. © Oxford Scientific Films

**Figure 1.20**
The orientation and exterior shape of the Compass Knoll reduces the entrance of sunlight into the interior. In the mornings the termites move to the western side, changing to the eastern side in the afternoon.

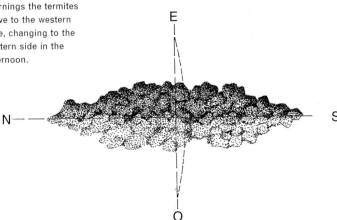

**Figure 1.22**
(a) Termite nest; (b) ecological house. In the case of both the termite nest and the ecological house, when hot air enters through a duct, it cools as it passes through the thermal earth mass, causing the hot air to rise and exit.

(a)

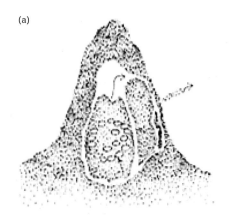

(b)

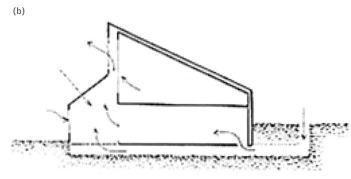

**Figure 1.23**
Design by André Bloc.

from this chamber and lead to thousands of compartments used as storerooms or living quarters. From the outside, the only obvious signs are small perforations that provide ventilation. The knoll also has rain gutters to remove excess water from the outside eaves. Nature presents termites with challenges, which they have overcome. We should take similar advantage of natural instincts in our architecture.

These amazing insects use a kind of passive, climatic architecture based on ventilation which allows them to renew the oxygen in their chambers. Some thousand litres of oxygen are circulated daily in order to eliminate the toxic carbon dioxide. One kind of termite in southern Africa has managed this by leaving a basement in the inner part and having an open space, like an attic, above it. The external wall of the knoll has a series of ruts or ducts through which the internal heat generated by the insects and the fungus they cultivate there may escape. The continual flow of hot air rises to the 'attic', enters the tubular ducts, passes through the lower storeroom, and leaves the knoll. The current again descends and circulates fresh air. The flow of stale air through the ducts facilitates the loss of carbon dioxide, while the thinness of the walls and ducts allows gaseous diffusion, keeping the internal temperature at 29° Celsius when the external temperature is often much higher. This is essentially the same principle as a convection heater.

It's essential for termites in arid regions to control humidity. They dig vertical tunnels in the sand, sometimes up to 40 metres deep, in search of water that can then ascend to their shelter through evaporation, thereby creating nearly 100 per cent humidity, even when the external air is completely arid. Other termites maintain ideal levels of humidity by cultivating fungi inside the nest; besides serving as food, these fungi produce heat when they grow, which absorbs any excess humidity by diffusing it into the air. Corridors and chambers are kept meticulously clean and constantly separated – and this within a population of millions of blind termites! This design is amazing and could be used in our own design of future self-sufficient ecological dwellings or for the development of bio-climatic dwellings, combined with eco-techniques such as solar energy and recycling water and waste. These would all help to maintain balance in our ecosystem.

## Amphibian Space: the Beaver's Lodge

The beaver more than justifies the title 'builder of nature' through its semi-aquatic home. Long before humans, these animals were dominating firm, solid spaces within different waters – ponds, channels, lagoons, rivers, streams – creating dwellings well protected from enemies and cold conditions, and for food storage. These extremely capable carpenters use only their bodies as tools. Their large, sharp teeth gnaw and cut, while the front feet are used to push firmly. Their small digits keep sticks and branches in place, and their hind feet are like fins. The tail can push down and transport small trees and also act as a rudder when swimming.

Beavers identify sites to build their community along the edges of water currents and close to trees. Once they've found a suitable place, they begin on the infrastructure. They start by redirecting the stream, damming it with wooden spikes which they've already connected to each other. During the night they gnaw at nearby trees, sculpting the trunks in the shape of sand clocks (timers) until they break. These tree trunks are then deposited in channels approximately 35 centimetres deep and 1.25 metres wide, which they dredged beforehand, so they can float to their destination. Once the tree trunks arrive, the beavers begin to build the dyke. The trunks are well anchored in the muddy bottom, forming a fence; the spaces between the trunks are afterwards filled with sticks and mortar made of clay and leaves.

If the current is fast and strong and the volume of water threatens the structure, the dyke is given a convex contour in the direction of the dam, which is just what engineers do to give greater resistance. On the top part of this wall, the beavers leave small holes or spillways to avoid disaster during seasons when the water level rises. The monitoring of water levels and the maintenance of the dam are the constant work of three or four generations. Occasionally, a large dam will be used for up to a 100 years.

The next step is to build the lodge itself. This is built upstream a short distance from the dam, over a small mound which is either natural or formed by the beavers using the same materials (sticks, branches, trunks, earth, and mud). The living quarters have one to several underwater tunnels leading up to a chamber which, when finished, will be above water level.

Beavers reach their lodge by swimming underwater and entering through the tunnels. They are therefore able to protect themselves from predators such as bears, who cannot get in. This hollow inside has a narrow chimney providing good ventilation. The floor of the lodge is carpeted with shavings of dry wood and bark that keep its inhabitants warm. To keep the floor in optimum condition, the beavers gnaw on wood inside the dwelling itself as often as necessary.

**Figure 1.24**
Cross-section of lodge and dam built by beavers.

The outside of a lodge reflects the inside. Generally, lodges have a conical or dome-like shape approximately 1.8 metres in diameter by 70 centimetres high on the inside; outside they may be 5 metres in diameter and 1.5 metres in height. Once building is finished, water is allowed to enter at calculated levels, filling the desired spaces. Beavers constantly repair breaks, leaks or damage produced over time.

Wood is the beaver's preferred food. To ensure survival during the winter, they store large quantities that can be carried to the lodge through the underwater tunnels, keeping a reserve, of which most will be used to feed the young. Older beavers live off accumulated fatty deposits and need very little other sustenance.

In the future, underwater cities could be planned on the same principles as those of the beaver's lodge. It should also be possible to exploit diverse marine resources and use hydraulic energy in marine waters. Access to the city would be possible by means of underwater tunnels, ancient Atlantis thereby becoming a reality for modern people.

It would be interesting to be able to watch animals build cities and houses for people. Through careful observation we can learn from their engineering and architecture. The cathedral in Brasilia, designed by the architect Oscar Niemeyer, is based on some of the principles of beaver construction, sharing similar concepts of function, space, structure, and form. Outside, the cathedral is surrounded by water. Its outer wall, which is concave, acts as a dam. To enter the building, one must go through a dark, narrow tunnel shaped like a ramp which emerges into an open, light space; it gives one the impression of coming out of an enormous cave.

**Figure 1.25**
Interior of the
Cathedral in Brasilia.
Oscar Niemeyer.

## Structure in nature

In the animal, vegetable and mineral kingdoms, fantastic structures help us to understand the basics of structural concept, which is, without doubt, the backbone of the creative constructive design within our architecture. Sometimes this produces friction between the architect and the structural engineer, especially at crucial moments of decision and agreement. A good architect should have a general knowledge of structure and spatial distribution, constructive aspects, mechanical and electrical systems, finances, a culture's social and psychological conduct, urbanism, history, theory of design, and so on.

Architects tend to have integral knowledge, engineers tend to have specialised knowledge. The latter 'know a lot about nothing', while the former 'know nothing about everything.' Clients may be fortunate enough to have an architect who understands structure and an engineer who appreciates aesthetics. The aesthetic and the technical are frequently at odds with each other, yet integrating the two may be more likely to result in something which satisfies our physical and spiritual needs better.

> 'We learn from the swallows how to construct homes, and we learn to sing from both the lark and the swan...'
> Democritus

**Figure 1.26 (left)**
Cathedral in Brasilia, Access ramp. Oscar Niemeyer.

The master builders of antiquity rarely had a thorough knowledge of theoretical precepts. They relied on empirical intuition about the structural fundamentals of pure physics. In this way it is possible to perceive how columns of a building must be wider at the bottom than the top, because they support the accumulated weight of all the floors of the structure, or how an arch functions.

In order to make calculations you need to have a structural design. Structural design should determine the form and proportion of the structure. It requires imagination, intuition, experience and knowledge.

With only a little theoretical knowledge, one can still know that a corbel supporting a balcony is well designed if the stilt decreases, but not well designed if the springing is higher than the apparent level of the impost because it seems to go against the laws of nature.

Structure represents one of many aspects of human creativity and cannot be imagined without a profound respect for natural laws. From a structural point of view, skeletons of four-footed animals are a system of double projection in which stresses balance themselves. This principle can also be applied to most ground transportation. The upper member of the projection is submitted to traction while in the body of the quadruped, the ligament works under tension and the skeleton under compression.

Another example is in the Sahuaro cactus. This reinforced, edifice-like plant stays upright, surviving winds, hurricanes and earthquakes through a combination of fibres that lend rigidity and work under tension, transmitting energy to the small root. The striated ribs on the outside also make it rigid. This plant inspired Frank Lloyd Wright the very first time he saw it.

In the construction of bridges or buildings with large openings or gaps, the structure is like the spinal column. Robert Maillart's bridges, based on a simple but clear idea, are beautiful examples of engineering executed with common sense. Their shape follows the function of frugality in construction. Maillart is important in the much-needed re-encounter of engineering with beauty. His works are found principally in the remote valleys of the Swiss Alps, linking areas separated by chasms: **'classic, agile leaps that save them.'**

**Figure 1.27**
The Salgina Tobel Bridge built by Robert Maillart (1929–1930), outstanding for its beautiful lines and its integration with the landscape.

Maillart, like the sculptor Constantin Brancusi, defined his creative principle with one word: economy. The limited financial resources of the small Swiss villages determined that: '**in order to construct a bridge, it had to be proved that it was more economic than any other.**'[27] According to Felix Candela: '**Maillart limited himself to a few shapes and basic ideas that he never abandoned; they required the whole course of one life to be developed to their ultimate and total perfection.**' The work of Robert Maillart is an important step towards the integration of two professions which should no longer be divorced: architecture and engineering.

It is convenient to see the work of later engineers, such as Eduardo Torroja, Santiago Calatrava or Felix Candela, and their hyperbolic paraboloid structures, as the continuation of this re-encounter between engineering and art initiated by Maillart.

The big goal of structure and the ideal solution for design problems lie in obtaining the greatest by way of the least. Structure does not consist of making something stronger or adding mass and volume, but of using material in the most suitable way. Without economising in structure, neither a bird with large, hollow bones nor an aeroplane could fly – they would both fall and perhaps they'd not even be able to take off in the first place. In the same way, without economising on materials, neither bridge nor tree could support its own weight.

The difference between synthetic and organic structures lies in the fact that the former (as a human product) helps us, while the latter is indispensable to every living organism.

## Structural Principles

There is no choice: humans must apply structure to buildings. Bridges exemplify typical structures in nature: the beam bridge made by a fallen tree; the arch bridge created by the erosion of rocks; and the hanging bridge formed by different types of vine. These three structural principles have remained unchanging for thousands of years.

**Figure 1.28**
Reserve Bank in Minnesota. In this building three structural principles can be observed that use nature to overcome clearings: the simple supports, the arch, and the hanging. Gunner Birkerts, 1968.

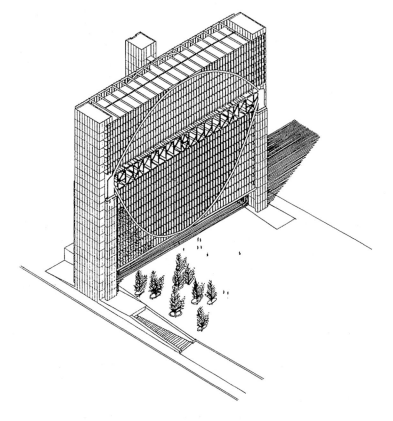

**Figure 1.29**
Different types of bridges found in nature: a) simply upheld; b) arch; c) hanging.

**Figure 1.30**
Types of bridges elaborated by humans: a) simply upheld; b) arch; c) hanging.

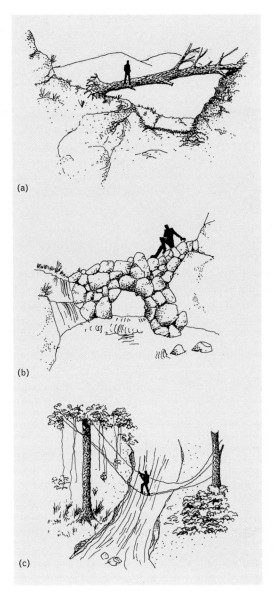

(a)

(b)

(c)

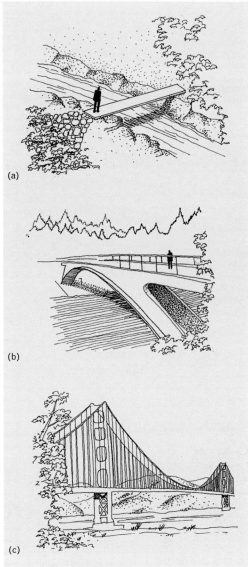

(a)

(b)

(c)

Everything contains a structure in itself. A structure's purpose is to transmit forces towards solid bases, usually land. This is the case for trees, bridges, buildings, or whatever. The forces that act on the structure produce five basic types of stress: compression, tension, flexion, cutting and torsion.

The tree is a good example of all five stresses at work. The upper surfaces of the wood fibres tense in the branches. Gravity pushes the branches downwards while the fibres on the lower surface compress. Flexion is produced inside the wood when gravity attracts the branches; when the wind bends them, torsion is produced. A cutting force is also generated during movement between the wood fibres, caused by the branches and trunk swaying in the wind.

Generally speaking, structures that undergo compression are short and thick. In order to support its great weight, pillars, something like an elephant's legs, gravitate outwards vertically from a point on the body close to its centre of gravity. Conversely, structures that use tension are slim and fragile, like cobwebs. These structures can support more weight with less material.

Imagine that an insect grows considerably larger than it does in real life. Its legs would have to be shorter and thicker to cope with the increase in weight; its wings would also have to

**Figure 1.31**
Longitudinal cross-
section of a thigh
bone. The
distribution of the
fibres at both ends
gives the bone its
required flexibility.

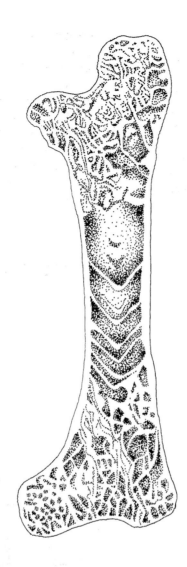

and tendons are tensed and the bones are compressed. A structure that is too rigid will break more easily than one that is flexible or elastic. What would happen if a team of human skeletons played football? They'd almost certainly be fractured before the end of the first half.

The human body's structural resistance can be explained through the linkage of all structural systems hard and soft, rigid and flexible, those that tolerate pressure, and those that resist it.

Theoretical calculus tends to separate traction and compression, but in reality this is not possible. People are now seeking materials that will offer as much resistance as possible to both. Cartilage is an example of a material that resists the stresses of compression and tension up to a point, helping to maintain the shape of some organs like the ears and nose.

The example of a tree will help further in our understanding of structure. The stresses (weight) of the highest branches (corbel) are transmitted downwards, increasing until they reach the trunk (spinal column), which transmits these stresses downwards (compression), increasing until they reach the ground. After that these stresses (weight) are transmitted into the ground through the roots (foundation). The roots contribute to the tree's well-being and balance by collecting rainwater that drips off surrounding plants.

The basic principles of continuity and fluidity in structures and in city planning and installations are also found in the vegetable kingdom, in trees and in cacti. In the mineral kingdom they are found in riverbeds and abundantly flowing rivers. In the animal kingdom they are found in the circulatory system.

City planning should consider the principle of the continuous flow that rivers develop. The small ones (side streets) widen little by little until they get to the main river (main road), which then flows into the delta (parking lot or trunk road).

We can also use the circulatory system as a model. The heart pumps blood through the arteries, which get narrower and narrower until they reach the capillaries, which join the venous system. The blood is then channelled at obtuse angles. This same principle of applying pressure to energy is found in the hydraulic system which uses a pump, the electrical system which uses a generator, and the air-conditioning system which uses a compressor. The pipes, cables or thick ducts become narrow, avoiding right angles or sharp angles that cause loss of energy through friction.

undergo modifications. If an elephant decreased in size its weight would be less and so it would no longer need such thick legs and feet for support.

The human body is an example of design in dynamic balance. The skeleton is the internal structure of the body, the basis of which is the backbone supported by the pelvis. The whole structure is held together and moved by the muscular system: ligaments, membranes, tendons, and muscles – a whole network in tension. Almost all long bones need to be flexible at both ends and rigid in the middle. Stresses are distributed through the use of internal fibres that range in consistency from soft to hard – they allow some animals, such as cats, to perform amazing movements during which the muscles

## Light Structures

Throughout the history of architecture, especially early on, great interest has been taken in the models for structures that nature offers. At the end of the twentieth century, technological advances and research by some architects and engineers has made it possible to build lighter structures on the same bases as those of the natural world. One of the greatest achievements in the fields of architecture and engineering is in the development of lightweight structures.

Scientists have studied light stable structures such as bones, insect and mollusc shells, skins and larger shells. The skeleton of a dinosaur, for example, inspired Professor Frei Otto to build a crane. The technique looks for constructional models based on light, stable structures.

In biology, Frei Otto found a fertile field of research for seeking resistant and rational structures. Japanese biologists apply such results in planning the growth of urban structures.

**Figure 1.32**
(a and b)
Arrangements of branches, ramifications.

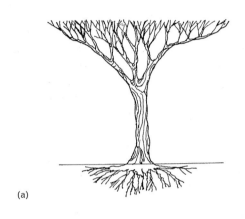

(a)

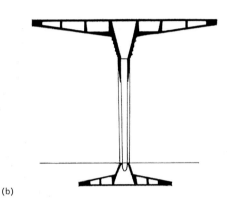

(b)

**Figure 1.33**
(a) River confluence; (b) circulatory system.

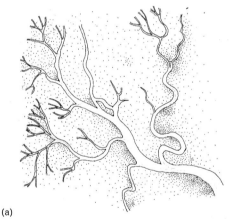

(a)

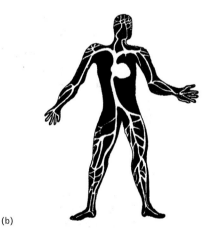

(b)

**Figure 1.34**
Principles of fluidity and continuity applied by humans to their (a) buildings and (b) infrastructure.

(a)

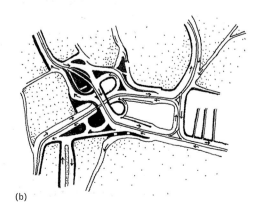

(b)

In the first buildings, designers generally 'copied' natural structures in an obvious way. These days, the sustaining structures of earlier models are being studied to create new designs. Such structures may help to develop an architecture capable of covering new spaces for humans.

There are basically four light structures derived from natural models:

| | |
|---|---|
| cable networks: | inspired by spiders' webs |
| pneumatics: | inspired by bubbles |
| vaults: | inspired by shells and eggs |
| geodesics: | inspired by radiolarians |

These light structures are characterised by low-cost materials, low dead weight, the possibility of large clearings, the simplification of constructive details, simple assembly, and short building time.

### Cable Networks

Spiders produce elastic, resistant webs with a minimum amount of material and at phenomenal speed. These viscous-elastic structures absorb impact and resist the struggles of insects without breaking, providing prototypes for 'new structures.' The static principles used in building

a web are the same as those used in 8000 BC by nomadic tribes making tents from animal skins to protect themselves from the wind.

The following example shows how wind can be neutralized. A handkerchief which is held out of the window of a moving car will vibrate, but if two of its opposite corners are stretched upwards and the other two stretched downwards, it becomes stable, and tightening will prevent wrinkles. This represents double curvature, commonly known as a saddle.

Our ancestors used a skin covering that sheltered small areas to protect themselves from the elements. Later, they designed a primary structure with synthetic materials. Later still, to shelter in larger spaces, they designed a network of cables as the principle structure, covering it with a membrane in materials such as acrylic, canvas and fibreglass.

In 1950, the architect Matthew Nowicki designed the first network of cables. This project was created for Cow Palace, Raleigh, North Carolina, USA, and was based on the same principle as the typical movie director's chair: a cloth membrane supported by four legs of crossed

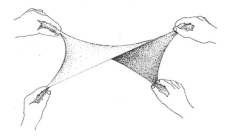

**Figure 1.35**
Double curvature or 'saddle.'

**Figure 1.36**
Cow Palace, Raleigh, North Carolina, USA. Matthew Nowicki, 1952.

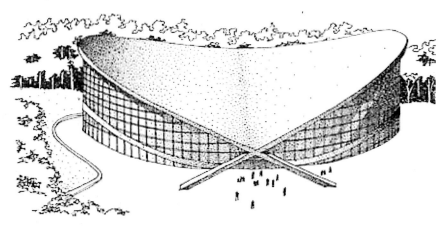

wood, pivoted at their half-way point, two at the front and they back.

Nowicki's construction uses reinforced concrete arches pivoted at both intersections. The cable network is tightened in two directions: some cables curved upwards parallel to the legs of the arches, others hang down perpendicular to the others. This structure turned out to have the shape of a saddle. All the cables are stretched with the weight of the arches which hang over

**Figure 1.37**
Network of cables,
Canadian Pavilion in
Osaka, 1970.

**Figure 1.38**
Detail of a spider's
web.

(a)

**Figure 1.39**
(a) Entrance to the
hockey rink at Yale
University. Eero
Saarinen, 1956–1950;
(b) hockey rink at
Yale University.

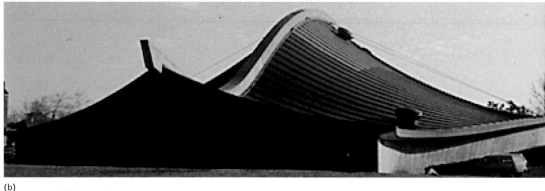

(b)

the same braces. Finally, the framework is covered with a network of wavy acrylic domes.

Let us now discuss the hockey rink at Yale University (1956–1958). Have you seen a hockey player skating at full speed over the ice? Have you ever wondered what tilt, what aerodynamics, what rhythm is required? Influenced perhaps by such an image, or by simple coincidence or a fortunate association of ideas, Eero Saarinen built a concrete arch as the main part of a structure that serenely crosses the whole shell. The dorsal column (arch) where the vertebrae (steel cables) are secured is very liberal indeed. These vertebrae hang in a perpendicular fashion like a hammock and are anchored in the walls, curved and slanted outwards. These walls work like dead weights, staking that anchor down, and at the same time working like counterweights for the roof. In this way the architect was able to achieve balance of the cables as if they were lengths of silk with a beautiful fall.

The entrances, enormous gullets that appear to devour the crowds, are arranged hierarchically by the projection of the roof, becoming a sort of corbel. Inside there is a simple and sobering elegance. The elements of the roof can be distinguished: the steel cables, the wooden lining that covers the ceiling looking like the hull of a ship, and the concrete of the arch... all of these take on a clean and harmonious appearance.

Saarinen also designed the roof of Dulles Airport in Washington, DC, USA. The cables hang in only one direction from the top of columns tilted outwards to raise the cable roof with prefabricated slabs, which in their turn keep

**Figure 1.40**
Dulles Airport,
Washington, DC,
USA. Eero Saarinen,
1960–1962.

the columns from falling. In this way, balance of forces is achieved in the structure.

Among other structures based on a cable network is the Sports Palace in Tokyo (1964) designed by Kenzo Tange (see Figure 1.72). It is built in a spiral shape around a central mast of sculptural concrete. Cables that are anchored to the bottom part of the bleachers hang from this central mast, while at the same time functioning as dead weight.

Another example of Olympic installations solved by cable network is the roof of the stadium in Munich, Germany, built for the 1972 Olympic

Games (Fig 1.41). The principles of resistance here are the same as those seen in a spider's web.

*Pneumatics*

In nature a great many forms are made up of micro-spheres (pneumatic structures). The micro-sphere behaves like a soap bubble in water, with a consistently flexible and resistant layer around a watery or gaseous content. Every animal or plant cell is a pneumatic structure made up of membranes and contents – the protoplasm. One of the fundamental properties of liquids is surface tension, the strength of which gives shape to

**Figure 1.41**
Another example of a
cable network. The
Olympic Stadium in
Munich. Frei Otto,
1972.

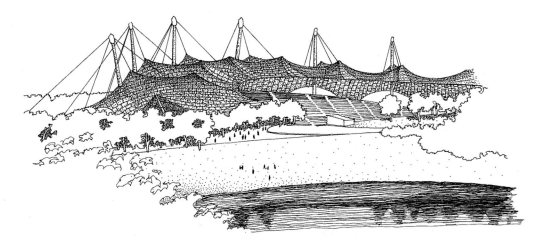

**Figure 1.42**
Inflated throat of a tree frog.

In toads that inflate their throat, the air behaves as an element of compression acting inside the membrane in tension (cf. Figure 1.42). The use of air as a structural material is, therefore, not new. In everyday life there are pneumatic structures in which air inside a resistant, protective shell-like covering supports a heavy weight. Such is the case of vehicle tyres, air mattresses, inflatable toys, sails inflated by wind, balloons, balls, and so on.

The pneumatic covering – *pneuma*, Greek for lung – is always soft. The original cells of wood and bone are actually soft but accumulate solid material like the bony or cellulose substances, becoming rigid 'pneumatic structures' that can hold up under certain pressure.

typical soap bubbles. When the bubble presents minimal surface, its shape results from a minimal amount of material. Besides being resistant, these light, flexible structures attain great plasticity.

We could consider ourselves pneumatic structures susceptible to puncture by sharp objects. Other examples of such structures are found in the conduction systems of plants: in viscera in general (the placenta, intestines, heart, stomach and lungs); in soft fruit such as grapes, tomatoes, and kernels of corn; in egg-yolks or the soft eggs of insects and reptiles.

It is no accident that the forms of pneumatic constructions developed by humans resemble natural shapes. Some of the techniques of abstract mathematics have slowly been lost as time has elapsed. Nevertheless, the result is still getting closer to the shapes found in organic life. Over the past three decades, air has become recognised as an important component of many structures.

At Expo '70 in Osaka, Japan, Yutaka Muramata designed the Fuji Pavilion (see Figure 1.43). It was built in 16 sections, each section being 4 metres wide. The perimeter measured 50

**Figure 1.43**
Fuji Pavilion. Yutaka Muramata, 1970.

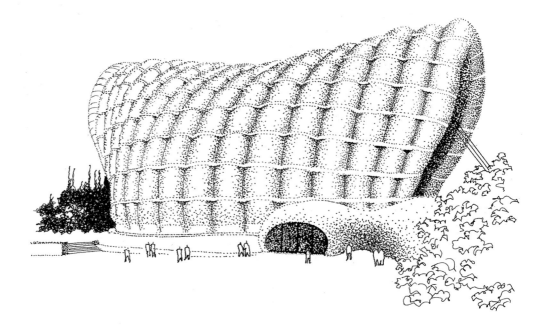

**Figure 1.44**
United States
Pavilion in Osaka,
Japan. David Geiger,
1970.

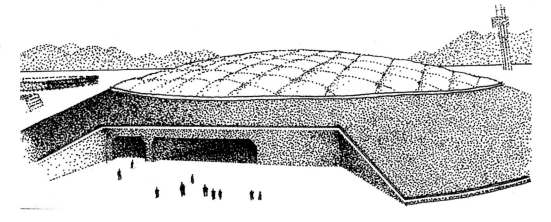

**Figure 1.45**
(a) The human
cranium; (b) thoracic
vault of a human
being; (c) the
skeleton of a seagull.

metres, and the Pavilion was 25 metres high.
When the inside pressure was increased, the
building was able to resist winds of hurricane
intensity.

David Geiger conceived an idea for the roof
of the United States Pavilion, in spite of serious
budget limitations (Figure 1.44). The roof
measures 87 metres by 53 metres and is made of
a vinyl membrane reinforced with fibreglass,
anchored to an oval-shaped, tilted wall. When
the membrane is inflated, the suspended cables
begin to tighten. The roof is held up by an air
pressure of 136.36 kilos per square centimetre
and can resist winds of up to 240 kilometres per
hour.

One of the largest roofs in the world, built in
1980 with reinforced cables, is a membrane made
of Teflon with fibreglass that covers the
Silverdome Stadium in Pontiac, Michigan, USA.
The roof, designed to reduce the original estimated
cost, hangs from a polygonal compression ring at
the highest point on the outside of the bleachers
and can cover 80,400 spectators.

### Vaults

One of the most interesting structures in nature is
the egg. Its shell is associated with two specific
properties: curved shape and hardness of
material. The shells of nuts such as pecans,
almonds or coconuts; crustaceans; the external
bodies of insects; and the pods of numerous seeds,
are similar. These natural structures generally
have greater rigidity than flat structures. They
protect life yet use a minimal amount of material.

Inside the human body, curved structures
protect vital organs. The cranium protects the

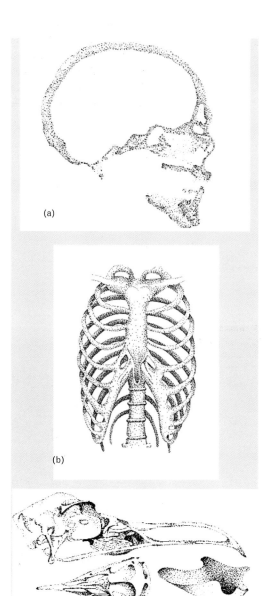

(a)

(b)

(c)

brain, and the thorax (more properly the thoracic vault) protects the heart, lungs, and other organs. The same is true of the central bone structure of a bird, which has similarities to a shell – it is nearly transparent and rigid – and serves as armour to protect internal organs.

Mollusc shells provide protection from predators, and their consistency means that they can withstand water pressure at depths.

The strength of a shell can be explained by the design of its structure: a thin plate with a curved surface that transmits stress throughout itself towards the supports. Shells can be built either with mouldable materials (clay, concrete, plastic) or from other materials (wood, metal, brick or stone) which can be put together and shaped into curved surfaces.

Shells of all materials support enormous pressures, due to their shape. The classic example is the egg, which has a very thin shell but, because of its continuous, double, curved shape, resists tremendous uniform pressures. Eggs are formed within the bird's body as spheres (pneumatic structures). The shell does not harden until the bird begins to push it out, when the spherical shape is modified to an oval shape. Inside the egg the yolk maintains its initial spherical shape as the shell and the albumin of the egg white protects it. Birds can then sit on their eggs without fear of breaking them because stress is evenly distributed throughout the shell.

Structural principles of the shell are the same in architecture as they are in nature – a curved, three-dimensional shape of rigid material and minimal thickness under the law of maximum efficiency and minimal material. Some spectacular large roofs built using this method are resistant, due exclusively to their shape.

**Figure 1.46**
Eggs.

*If you hold a sheet of paper by one edge, it cannot support its weight. If you curve one of its ends upwards with the other hand, the paper will become rigid and will act like a sloping corbel. It will be able not only to support its own weight, but to hold a pen, say, as well. It becomes rigid by curving one side upwards, not by adding extra material to it. This principle of rigidity through curvature is efficiently applied to projecting roofs of reinforced concrete 10 metres or more with a thickness of no more than a few centimetres.*

**Figure 1.47**
A concrete shell. The Kresge Auditorium at M.I.T. Eero Saarinen, 1953–1956.

**Figure 1.48**
Examples showing an increase of rigidity through the use of curved forms: (a) sheet of paper; (b) leaf of tree; (c) roof.

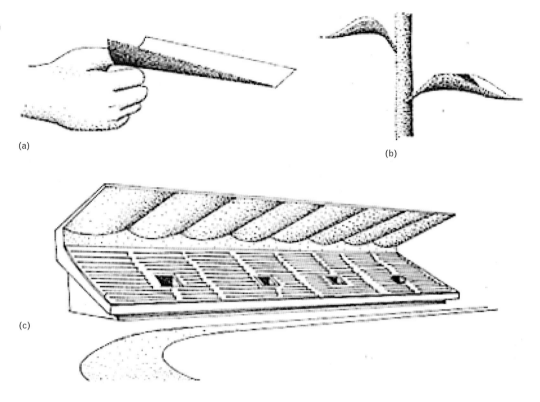

(a)

(b)

(c)

The flatter the curvature of a shell, the less load it can hold; the greater the curvature, the greater the load it can hold. In this way, shells can be architecturally classified into four different types: roof arches, with single curvature (Figure 1.49a); domes, with double curvature (Figure 1.49b); hyperbolic paraboloids, with double, inverse curvature (Figure 1.49c); and free forms, a combination of all three (Figure 1.49d).

*To demonstrate consistency, the barrel vault (with curvature in one direction) must remain correctly supported (embedded). You can check this for yourself by covering the space between two books with a sheet of paper: if you put the paper across the books as you would a tile, the paper will fall, but if you curve the paper upwards and it is propped up on the cover of each book so that it is secure, it will stay in position. The curvature gives the paper a new consistency if the sheet is rolled up, transforming it into a rigid tube similar to the large wing bones of birds, which resist strong flexibility momentums. It also resembles bamboo, which tolerates bending due to articulated rings that reinforce the stem.*

Domes represent yet another kind of shell. To understand stresses that are transmitted in a dome, apply pressure to the upper part of an eggshell. The compression stresses become tension as they reach the edges and crack. This difficulty is solved when constructing a dome by using a ring (under tension) reinforced with steel, or a tie beam that reduces the stress (Figure 1.50). Generally speaking, these domes of double curvature can resist twice as much, or more, than barrel vaults with curvature in only a single direction. At present, with the use of more

**Figure 1.49**
Different types of shells: (a) barrel vault; (b) dome; (c) hyperbolic paraboloid; (d) free form.

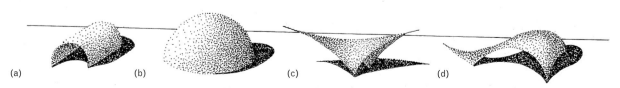

(a)

(b)

(c)

(d)

**Table 1.1 Variations between structural forms of buildings old and new**

| Structure | Clearing (height of the dome) | Thickness of the dome | Ratio of thickness/clearing |
|---|---|---|---|
| St. Peter's Cathedral Rome, Italy | 40.00 m | 3.00 m | 1:13 |
| Church of Our Lady of Dresden, Germany | 24.00 m | 1.25 m | 1:19 |
| Zeiss Planetarium Jena, Germany | 40.00 m | 6.00 cm | 1:66 |
| Basel Market Basel, Switzerland | 60.00 m | 8.50 cm | 1:70 |
| Hen's egg | 4.00 cm | 0.40 mm | 1:100 |
| Exposition Salon Paris, France | 205.00 m | *13.00 cm | 1:570 |

*13 cm is the sum of both domes measuring 6.5 cm of the double shell.
© Curt Siegel, *Structural Forms of Modern Architecture* (1967).

**Figure 1.50**
(a) Illustration of the difference a ring under tension makes to the resistance of an eggshell (dome). (b) Chapel in Lomas de Cuernavaca, Guillermo Rosell and Manuel Larrosa. Examples showing the arched false work, reinforcement and layer of 4-centimetre thick concrete which covers the 'crests.' Structural design, Felix Candela, 1959.

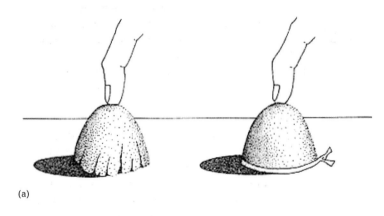

(a)

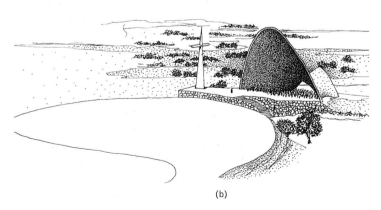

(b)

efficient materials, it is possible to reduce the thickness of structures for roofs and overcome clearings as shown in Table 1.1, taken from the book *Structural Forms of Modern Architecture*, which explains differences in the quantity of material used to build the old domes constructed with masonry as compared with today's domes which have the natural shape of an egg.

Another variety of shell shapes is the hyperbolic paraboloid designed by Felix Candela in Mexico during the 1950s and 1960s, which covers churches, gas stations and warehouses, among other things. The relative simplicity of design and construction is due to the use of straight elements (ruled surfaces) to form a double inverse curvature. The construction of a saddle is a classic example.

Colin Faber points out: '**During his career Candela began to gather everything that had been written on shells, seashells, and eggshells and to study their resistance to pressure, why they do not break, and so on.**'[28] Several years later during the most productive phase of his life, Candela commented: '**It was as if everything that had happened before in my life began to make sense in a completely meaningful way. I began to feel in shape, like an athlete, and mentally I also felt that the time had come to do something.**'[29]

Candela did not favour meticulous and detailed calculations, or at least he did not base his work on them. At certain stages of his life, he blindly trusted intuition: '**When I began**

**Figure 1.51**
(a and b) The *Manantiales* restaurant in Xochimilco, Mexico D.F. Joaquín and Fernando Alvarez Ordóñez. Examples showing the arched false work, reinforcement and layer of 4-centimetre thick concrete which covers the 'crests.' Structural design, Felix Candela, 1957–1958.

(a)

(b)

constructing roofs, my mind was barely leaving the student stage. As students we believe everything we are told. For example, we believe we have exact methods to calculate structures. At that moment I began to lose faith in everything I had previously believed. This is a necessary starting point for anyone who is going to make something of his own.'[30] Every good teacher should applaud this statement by Candela.

The crests of bivalves, like the wrinkles or creases that pass towards the inner part of a shell, increase rigidity and resistance without increasing overall thickness too much. Structures can be resistant by being light in weight – like biological structures such as seashells – rather than by mass and reinforcement.

'What induced Candela to develop the free edge was merely aesthetics, a desire to take the essence of a shell and express it visually. Nothing could be subtracted from the Jacaranda nor the restaurant in Xochimilco. There is nothing more than the tense membranes of the roof' explains Colin Faber.[31] In this case, the clear and straightforward structure delineates space thereby achieving overall harmony. Referring to the *Jacaranda* nightclub (Figure 1.52), Faber tells us: 'The roof suggests a shape softened by the constant movement of the sea. When seen from the

**Figure 1.52**
The *Jacaranda* nightclub, Acapulco, Gro. Mexico. Juan Sordo Madaleno. Examples showing the arched false work, reinforcement and layer of 4-centimetre thick concrete which covers the 'crests.' Structural design, Felix Candela, 1957.

roof of the hotel, it looks like a turtle that just came out of the water. Seen closer from the sea, it looks like the stretched, wind-filled sail of a boat.'[32] It is clear, then, that the greatness of Candela is based on his adapting natural forms to concrete.

The last variation of the shell is found in the free forms characterised by a combination of double curvature. The project of the architect Eero Saarinen for the TWA terminal in Kennedy Airport in New York City exemplifies a free structural design and represents a formal unit that is comparable to forms in nature.

Michel Ragon in his book *Where Shall We Live Tomorrow?* points out that: '**Eero Saarinen with his General Motors factory, called the Versailles of the twentieth century, had perfected the parallelepiped box of Mies van der Rohe, who changed the style completely a short while before his death... Following the school of Antoni Gaudí of Spain, he carries out his architectural work on the boundaries of expressionist sculpture. He conceives the idea of whirlpools starting from curved forms of concrete that suction and transport all the way to the vast shell of the interior where a comfortable and dramatic space is found... and in the word dramatic we include the ideas of surprise, mystery, and poetry.'**[33]

Eero Saarinen himself explained his designs: '**It could be said that it is all about structural forms that are derived from the laws of the curved shell. It is about an aesthetic will that seeks continuity in all architectural elements... The flow of all the elements makes it impossible to design it with drawings... The rehearsals will be made in the model all the way to the final solution... It was a happy day indeed when we finished the models. We found, for example, that there were marvellous, spontaneous forms in the plant that we would never have discovered on a drawing board.'**[34]

The outside form of the terminal evokes the figure of a bird just about to fly. However, according to Saarinen, he was far from thinking about such symbolism. In this case the structure is a determining factor in the expression of the form. This structure opens up new possibilities for encouraging architectural fantasy.

### Geodesics

The natural origin of the hexagon is found in bubbles or spherical cells: whether they're the cells of complex organisms, viruses, or whatever, when grouped together and compressed by crowding, they adopt hexagonal shapes the intersections of which form angles of 120° due to surface tension (Figure 1.54). This same pattern can be seen in the tortoise's shell and the giraffe's skin.

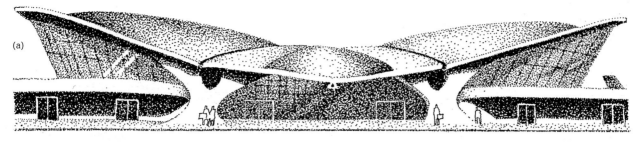

(a)

**Figure 1.53**
(a) TWA terminal at Kennedy Airport, N.Y. Eero Saarinen, 1958–1961; (b) horizontal section of the roof of the TWA building (left) compared to that of a Dictyonema (right, 200× natural size).

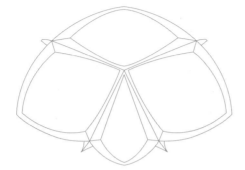

(b)

**Figure 1.54**
120° angles created between soap bubbles.

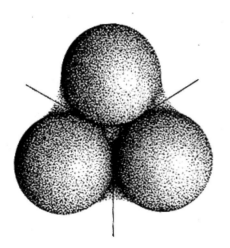

Radiolaria are microscopic planktonic or sedentary protozoan organisms; they are mostly marine but some are freshwater. A radiolarian has a generally spherical shape and is composed of skeletal silicon, strontium or chitin, complexly patterned and immersed within the overall cell content of protoplasm. Its skeletal network resembles the separation of the different bubbles, and superficial energy around the periphery sometimes leads to a hexagonal appearance, and sometimes to perforation through the skeleton by protoplasmic processes which trap passing food. This kind of spherical basket is similar to the most delicate Chinese ivory ball imaginable.

I do not know if Buckminster Fuller knew that the structure of the metacarpal bone of a vulture's wing is three-dimensional. However, he did know about the structures of radiolaria and diatoms and he was convinced that the most efficient network of constructive stress is constituted by the combination of a sphere with hexagons and triangles – the geodesic, which he invented.

It can also be found in the beehive. A simple worker bee starts to build a honeycomb by chewing scales and salivary secretion together to make tiny balls of waxy material that are then stuck to each other. Other bees copy this, thus beginning the process of shaping the cells, placing wax where needed and removing any excess so that a characteristic combination of cells is created. This phenomenon has always inspired philosophers, naturalists and mathematicians.

**Figure 1.55**
The metacarpal bone
of a vulture's wing.

A geodesic is a series of tetrahedrons that cannot be deformed and that form a sphere. This combination is rigid, light, clean, and uses few prefabricated elements, meaning that it can be built in a relatively short time and at a relatively low cost.

For Fuller the geodesic consisted of the constant refinement of a structure, in some cases giving way to a formalistic architecture. Felix Candela speaks about this in his book *In Defence of Functionalism and Other Writings*: '**The process is... contrary to the usual architectural projects. The structural form is chosen first, and afterwards you look to see if it is possible to integrate function.**'[35]

**Figure 1.56**
Geodesic Dome.
United States
Pavilion in Montreal.
Buckminster Fuller,
1967.

# Shape in nature

Generally speaking our first impression of an object comes through shape. In living organisms, form reflects the conditions and stages of life. In the epidermis, for example, you can see the body's internal functioning: paleness, ageing, beauty, obesity, and so forth. It is also a reflection of troubles, work, joys, the weight of years; every part of life is registered here. The force of gravity also influences the organism: we find it reflected in wrinkles, drooping breasts and sagging eyelids. Gravity is a strong factor in determining shape. In 1917, D'Arcy Thompson wrote: '**If the force of gravity were double what it is, our biped posture would be impossible and most earthly animals would look like lizards with short legs or like snakes... If gravity were reduced to half, on the other hand, we would acquire a lighter, more slender, active shape, we would need less warmth, less energy, less heart, lungs, and blood.**'[37]

The shapes of the feet and beaks of different birds give us a clear idea of their living environment, diet, and habits. The hardness of the ground make claws and talons necessary. The beak of a bird of prey is a sharp, curved hook for tearing meat. Birds that seek their food in swampy areas usually have long feet and beaks. Those that live in water have webbed feet to use as oars and to swim.

Environment determines shape. Giraffes, for instance, looking for food in treetops, developed a neck that became longer and longer with evolution.

Just as physical surroundings determine the shapes of living creatures, the way in which something is designed affects characteristics of architecture and its inhabitants. Shapes can be created from the inside out as well as from the outside in.

❝External configuration is generally quite simple, but packaged inside of a living organism, there is an amazing complexity of structures that has been the delight of anatomists❞

Robert Venturi, *Complexity and Contradiction in Architecture*[36]

**Figure 1.57**
Illustration of glass blower.

**Figure 1.58**
Diet and environment determine the shape of the beaks of birds.
© DigitalVision.

A glass blower creates shapes from the inside out. Using a simple, closed tube with a glass blister at one end, he blows evenly, tilting to one side or allowing one side of the bubble to cool more than the other, to make the required shape. In nature too, shape frequently begins with tubular structures. This can clearly be seen in the circulatory system, nervous system, brain, and digestive tract.

Organic development and growth generate as a result of coherent shapes manifest in living entities. This coherence is what designers strive for in order to obtain pleasing results. Designing from the inside out as much as from the outside in generates tensions that help to integrate the design.

There are times when looking at a shape can subconsciously give someone the necessary inspiration to solve a problem. Perhaps this explains what happened when Buckminster Fuller, seeing the shape that a drop of water took while falling, designed a car able to go faster because of its shape.

To summarise, function, space, structure and shape constitute a whole. Function requires space, space is limited by structure, and shape, in turn, reflects that structure. Shape is nothing more than the reflection of structure that limits the space that function requires.

At different periods of history, architectural design has leant on these four fundamental concepts, although some eras have emphasised them more than others. A rather more detailed analysis follows of a natural archetypical design in which function, form, structure and space constitute an integrated whole: the mollusc.

The snail

**Figure 1.59**
Microscopic view of a
six-day-old snail
embryo. © Alejandro
Martinez Mena.

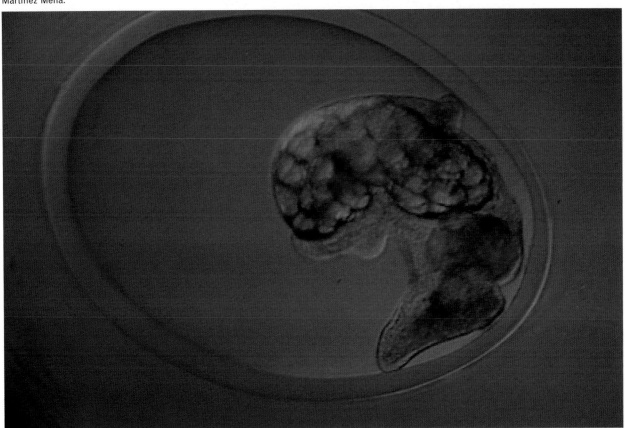

❛The architect of the future will build inspired by nature because it is the most rational, the most durable, and the most economic of all methods❜

Juan Torras (1810)[38]

## Snails, Clams and Cephalopods: Molluscs

### The snails, their nature

Snails are known scientifically as members of the Gastropoda (Mollusca). Molluscs mostly have shells, and snails belong to a group (phylum) which evolved on this planet some 500 million years or more ago.

The construction of the shell involves a process similar to that of the human fingernail. The shell is formed through secretions of the mantle glands that control its growth, form and colour. The secretion is a mixture of lime dissolved in water and enlarges the shell as and when the animal needs it. A mollusc doesn't have an internal skeleton, so this external shell acts like a skeleton but is also protective.

It is surprising how molluscs, being so soft, can create such hard, resistant structures. The shell is formed with knots, spines or thin sharp layers that give protection against predators. The structure grows and is enlarged gradually, consolidating itself progressively from inside. Ridges or folds appear, finally forming the spirals that characterise snail shells.

The growth of the mollusc shell is from the inside outwards. This type of growth is called intussusception. In the mineral kingdom, however, growth, whether it's an increase or decrease, is caused by the accumulation (or loss) of material from the outside, as in the cases of stalactites or the erosion of rocks. This is known as juxtaposition.

Externally, shells have grooves, smooth surfaces, fanciful textures, contrasting colours and/or both symmetrical and asymmetrical outlines. There are endless design possibilities. The inner layers of shells can be comparatively soft, porcelain-like, tinted with pale pink, white, or shades of blue or green. This is where the mother-of-pearl, a material widely used in cosmetics, industry, and jewellery, comes from.

Molluscs can be classified as terrestrial, parasitic, freshwater or marine. Marine molluscs can be simplistically divided into univalves and bivalves. The former have the shape of a single shell that is generally spiral, such as nautiluses, while the latter, such as clams, oysters and mussels, have two parts (valves) articulated by something like a hinge – formed of ligaments – that opens and closes the shell.

**Figure 1.60**
Cross-section of the *Nautilus*. (c)Aldi Oyarsabal.

### Univalve (cephalopod): Nautilus

Within this group is the legendary mollusc highly valued by people – the nautilus. The oldest fossils are around 350 million years old. Their characteristics have impressed many observers such as Leonardo da Vinci, who designed a submarine inspired by the basic characteristics of this extraordinary creature. Years later Jules Verne, in his book *Twenty Thousand Leagues Under The Sea* (1870), named his vessel 'The Nautilus' in its honour.

The outside of the shell has an ivory colour with brown spots; inside it glistens like mother-of-pearl. When it grows it constructs larger and larger chambers in a spiral arrangement by means of a curved tube located centrally throughout the chambers and connected to its digestive system. The last chamber built is the one the mollusc inhabits; it is the largest and the most secure. When this no longer fits, another chamber is built, the previous one being sealed off with a partition or septum. If attacked by a predator, it covers the entrance to the shell with a resistant, leather-like material (a hood).

The nautilus is capable of reaching considerable depths (greater than 500 metres), transporting itself by means of a propulsion system: it fills all its chambers with gas similar to air, creating buoyancy, and expels it through the curved central tube. The changes in pressure cause spiral movement. This is the same general principle used in submarines.

### Bivalve: Giant Clam

The Giant Clam, another legendary creature, belongs to this group. Armand Lendrin, in his text *The Book of Wonders* (1879), commented: '**It weighs very little (6 kilos) compared to its massive shell. Each valve in the shell reaches a weight of 250–350 kilos with a length of between 1 to 1.5 metres.**'[39]

Bachelard refers to this shell in the following terms: '**What a fantastic bath could be taken in the dwelling of such a mollusc! Who would not feel cosmically heartened and strengthened imagining himself bathing in the shell of The Great Basin?**'[40]

Bivalve shells have aroused great curiosity, as much for their shape as for what they shelter; one of the jewels we most prize is naturally produced within – the pearl. Most of these pearls are spherical and are formed by the slow entry of the microscopic eggs of small organisms. Sometimes a simple grain of sand is enough to stimulate the mollusc to produce a pearl. The great *Tridacna* (Giant Clam) can create pearls as big as golf balls over a ten-year period.

On the constructive abilities of the mollusc, Leonardo da Vinci once wrote: '**The creature that resides within the shell builds his dwelling with joints, ceilings, and several other parts... and this creature enlarges his house and roof gradually in proportion to his body's growth, adhering to the sides of the shell**'[41]

## The Spiral in Nature

Everything from microcosm to macrocosm turns spirally – it is the universal movement. In observations made with the most modern microscopes, the spiral occurs as much in mineral crystals as in the molecular structure of DNA. Similarly, movements of planetary systems and galaxies delineate paths in spirals. The spiral movement is found in the elements: waves in the ocean, volcanic eruptions on earth, whirling in air and fire.

**Figure 1.61**
Microscopic view of a crystal of ascorbic acid. Everything moves in a spiral, from the micro-cosmos to the macro-cosmos.

The spiral is the geometrical path that governs gastropods and other molluscs. A spiral is the trajectory that a physical line traces as it twists around again and again with an ever-increasing radius of curvature. The constant and the logarithmic spirals are the best known.

Archimedes' constant spiral, or screw, is characterised by the fact that in general, each turn conforms to the same separation as the one before. One example from nature is the spiral that the spider weaves after having stretched its frame with woven spokes.

In contrast, the logarithmic spiral, described for the first time by René Descartes in 1638, is best understood by rolling a rope around a cone. Two examples from nature illustrate this: the shape into which an elephant curls its conical trunk and the shape of a nautilus.

The spiral, because of its structural delineation, rhythm, feeling, and continuity, has awakened curiosity and inspiration, and much has been written about this geometrical pattern throughout the centuries.

Certain animals in nature exhibit a growing helicoid-spiral shape in their horns or fangs; this is repeated in the arrangement of segments in pineapple skin or the spiral shell of the nautilus already mentioned. Based on this growth process in nature, models of different dimensions or proportions, such as Fibonacci's series, the logarithmic spiral, or the golden section so defended by theorists and artists, were produced.

As María Teresa Piazza affirms: '**The spiral is the natural shape of growth and has come to be, in each culture and in each period of time, a symbol of the advance of the soul toward eternal life, making the journey to the very centre of the secret of life easier. Without the spiral we would be as vulnerable as a snail if his shell grew large and straight. Life's experiences twist around and protect us with speculations and anticipation. The universe and human conscience itself form a continuum and dynamic that can be rightly expressed in a spiral.**'[42]

Some philosophers believe that the spiral wraps our lives in time and space. A smell or sound, for instance, can sometimes transport us, mentally, to another place, another time. This coming and going, some humanists say, is produced by unclosed cycles. Following a spiral, we are returned to a nearby point, making life an infinite continuum.

Continuous or lineal time is a great lie. It is no accident that all the important religions of the world understand time to be recyclable. In the words of Mircea Eleade: '**Sacred time is by its own nature reversible, in the sense that in itself it is primordial, mythical time made present.**'[43] To go on is to get further away; to get further away is to return.

Sor Juana Inés de la Cruz (a seventeenth-century Mexican nun and poet) wrote: '**Two girls were playing with a spinning top in front of me... I had some flour brought and sifted to try to discover if the top spinning over the flour made perfect circles or not, and I found that they were not but spiral lines that slowly lost their circular form as momentum slackened.**'[44]

**Figure 1.62**
Descartes' spiral.

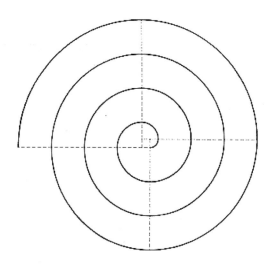

**Figure 1.63**
Archimedes' screw.

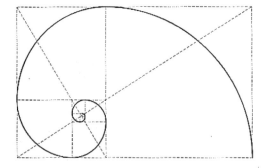

**Figure 1.64**
Close-up of a molluscan spiral. ©
Alejandro Martinez
Mena.

## Design in Gastropod and Cephalopod Molluscs

If, while planning an architectural design, we follow the principle of the growth of living organisms, we will delimit our space to that which its function requires, just as molluscs adjust their shells as required. The space built and adapted to the model will be comprised of multiple forms of double curvature with designs of different sizes, tubes curled around imaginary axes to infinity. Thoreau said: '**What I now see of beauty in architecture I know has been gradually developed from the inside out depending on the needs and character of those who dwell there.**'[45]

Some theorists on shape think that these spaces are ones that humans would ideally want to live in and own. Thus the shell represents an intimate boundary whose circularity gives us tranquillity. We have continually sought caves and hollows as shelter. Gaston Puel believed this firmly and wrote poetically:

'I will speak this morning
of the simple happiness of a man
tucked away in the hollow of a small
    boat.
The oblong shell of a canoe has closed
    over him.
He sleeps.
It is an almond.
The little boat, like a bed, embraces
    sleep.'[46]

**Figure 1.65**
Close-up of a spiral staircase, bell-tower in Atlantida. Eladio Dieste.

Modern humans lack the restful relaxation described in these lines, while nature rocks in peaceful harmony.

A mollusc is a harmonious whole. Harmony is achieved by an affinity or contrast of shapes. In the mollusc, the part goes with the whole just as the whole goes with the part. Using the mollusc as his model, the architect can design and build something based on the fundamental concepts of function, space, structure, and shape. The bases that architectural design rests on are also found in the design of the shell: character, equilibrium, volume, rhythm, contrast, protective colouring, monochromatic design, scale, proportion, continuity, harmony and unity. We can translate the space that the mollusc generates with its shape into feelings such as serenity, surprise, isolation, humility, joy and integrity.

Frank Lloyd Wright, when referring to the integrity essential to every architectural design, was of the opinion that a really beautiful building must necessarily be functional: **'An organically lovely house cannot help but be practical....'**[47] He also criticised the excessive usefulness of 'machines for living', affirming that 'they were ugly because they were created to make life easier.' In the same way that a mollusc creates a shape adaptable to its body, humans should create a living space for themselves in harmony with their characteristics. Lao Tsé used to say that: **'the reality of a house does not lie in its roof nor in its walls but in the space it encloses.'**[48]

The different components of shape should not be in discord. The architect, says Sullivan: **'should let a building develop in a natural way, logically and poetically, starting with its condition. The outside appearance should represent the inside appearance.'**[49]

The mollusc, with harmony and simplicity, reintegrates the three fine arts: architecture, sculpture, and painting. The integration of these three visual arts is called Arsculpain. Arsculpain can be found throughout the history of humanity in all spaces that humans have inhabited, such as the caves of Altamira in Spain, the Parthenon, the pre-Hispanic pyramids, and Gothic cathedrals. Not until modern times have people, in their eagerness to specialise, separated the artistic path of each of these three disciplines.

The mollusc maintains its shell lustre throughout its life. The colour of mollusc shells is no extravagance, but rather forms part of their very existence and varies according to the surroundings and temperatures in which they develop: the warmer the water, the brighter the colour; when the water is colder or the animal has died, the colours fade to white, due to a total absence of pigment.

**Figure 1.66**
Molluscs. Volume, rhythm, contrast, mimicry, continuity, and colour. Design concepts that blend.

**Figure 1.67**
Detail of the temple of Quetzalcóatl in Teotihuacán, Mexico where painting, sculpture, and architecture are integrated into a whole.

**Figure 1.68**
Volume, colour and texture are integrated with the landscape at 'Lovers' Fountain.' Luis Barragán.

Climate, therefore, determines the mollusc's colour – both its intensity and its shades. The form and colour of sky, sea, mountains, forests, or sunset make up the essence of the fine arts and all are related to temperature. At the North Pole, cool colours dominate the landscape: whites, greys, sky blue, and blue-green. The closer one travels towards the equator, the more one finds contrast, and when reaching the tropical zones, the colours become warmer: dark brown, chestnut, maroon, the red of the land, the ochre of sand, and the bright tones of flowers, which contrast with the blue of the sky and the sea and the green of trees.

Gaudí believed that in the Mediterranean area the people are more creative and more apt to use colour, whereas the Saxons are more reserved and cool, like their lands and waters. Gaudí defended the use of many colours, and he explained it in a book of memoirs that he wrote when 26 years old: '**Ornamentation has been,**

**Figure 1.69**
Turritella, Minaret.

is, and always will be coloured. **Nature provides us with nothing monochromatic... not in vegetation, nor in geology, nor in the animal kingdom. Colour contrast is always more or less alive, hence we should apply colour to part or all of an architectural structure,** colouring that will perhaps disappear so that the hand of time may apply another that is more appropriate and exact than the old one.'[50]

To colour is added texture. The surface that has been coloured – be it natural or artificial – presents smooth textures together with visual and tactile sensations. Molluscs and their shells offer us as many, if not more, textures as there are species. In the same way architecture, in order to reveal itself as such, should show its face and surface, coloured over a preconceived texture and created with imagination.

## Architectural Design Inspired by Molluscs

Throughout the ages the mollusc has been the object of inspiration for many cultures. The oldest known examples of molluscs in art are found in the cave paintings of France and Belgium. In the Americas the Mayas, Toltecs, Aztecs, and Incas used shells as symbols, tools, musical instruments, money, ornaments, and jewellery. This was the same in ancient Greece, India, and Africa. The Greeks borrowed the 'cupped' shape to achieve good acoustics and resonance in the design of their theatres.

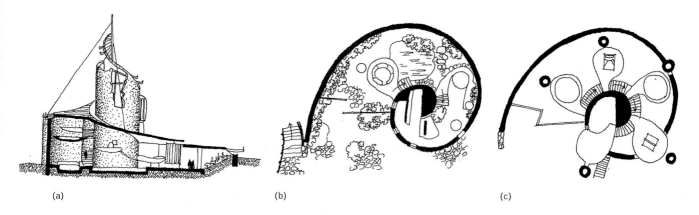

(a)                                    (b)                                    (c)

**Figure 1.70**
Bruce Goff was
inspired in the
delineation of the
logarithmic spiral for
the Bavinger House,
Norman, Oklahoma,
1951–1956. (a)
Elevation view; (b)
plan views.

Renaissance Europe embraced endless architectural shapes enriched with decorative elements associated with these creatures. Even religious art abounded in such shapes, which acquired symbolic connotations in altars, niches, as images of saints and as receptacles for holy water. It has been assumed that the mollusc was a hierofania or a divine manifestation since time immemorial. In painting, for example, we find it in Botticelli's 'The Birth of Venus' (c.1480). During the rococo style of the eighteenth century, the shell appeared in diverse arts, carefully and fancifully wrought with great imagination. In Arabia, Turritella shells inspired the minarets of Muslim mosques. In Salamanca, The House of Shells is famous for its carved stone façade decorated with bivalves (scallop shells, representing St James of Compostela).

During the period of the Flemish baroque, Rembrandt painted molluscs with great precision, beauty and naturalness. Miró and Picasso created paintings in which molluscs have the main role. Henry Moore sculpted pieces with shapes that announce the prolific presence of molluscs.

The balance between form and structure synthesised in the mollusc's shell represents a stimulating challenge for the architect. For practical reasons its characteristics have been adopted as principles for building the compressed vault and the curved structure, a prevailing element in Roman, Byzantine, Romanesque, Gothic, Renaissance and baroque architecture. This not only represents a great technical achievement but it also demonstrates the will to control space.

**Figure 1.71**
Opera House in
Sydney, Australia.
Jorn Utzon,
1959–1973.

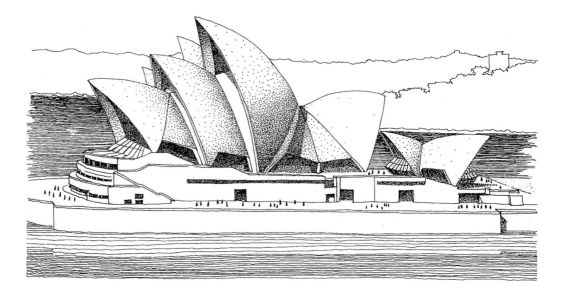

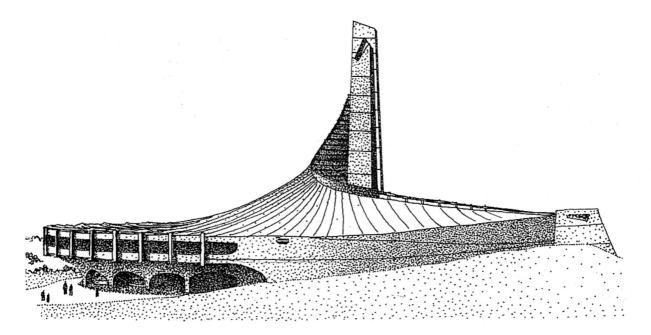

**Figure 1.72**
Sports Palace in
Tokyo. Kenzo Tange,
1964.

In contemporary architecture, Gaudí incorporated the spiral line into his columns, stairs and towers. Le Corbusier designed a museum with a spiral shape and continuous growth. Bruce Goff defined the structure of the Bavinger House with a long stone wall forming an ascending logarithmic spiral. Jorn Utzon designed the famous Opera House in Sydney, the source of much controversy, and Kenzo Tange built his marvellous shell-shaped structure for the Olympic Games in Tokyo.

Nevertheless, the most renowned architectural design based on natural principles of the mollusc form is the Guggenheim Museum. The architect, Frank Lloyd Wright, spent a great deal of his time studying molluscs, and designed a continuous living space in harmony with structure and form; one style, one colour and just one material. Its creator has said: '**Here, for the first time, is architecture made art. A floor joined with the one below instead of the well-known superposition of stratified layers cut and sustained by pillars and beams. The whole building, one solid mass of concrete, looks more like an eggshell on account of its extreme simplicity than an intercrossed structure... The light concrete matter is made solid enough at all points to do the job with the use of steel filaments embedded separately or as a screen. This revolutionary and completely artistic sense, which began as a mere instinct in me, started working increasingly intelligently with unforeseen and fascinating consequences.**'[51]

Wright also made this comment about molluscs: '**The dwellings of these primary lives of the sea are the houses we lack; it would be like living in a beautiful and naturally inspired way. Observe the innate capacity for invention revealed in this collection of minute residences built by hundreds of small, natural creatures. Each one has built its own house with a lovely, unmistakable variation that will never end.**'[52]

It would be difficult to over-estimate the importance of these small creatures to human art and imagination. A passage from the writings of Bernard Palissy (sixteenth century) cited in the *Poetics of Space* by Gaston Bachelard tells us that Palissy sought: '**in the forests, mountains, and valleys to see if he can find an industrious animal that has fabricated some industrious houses which will serve as a model in the formation of an idea concerning protective shelters against the threat of war. After a long search he finds the mollusc.**'[53] These soft creatures protect themselves from predation by other animals by means of their hard shell and Palissy based his ideas on this. The city fortress could be designed on the principle of spirals. In the very centre of the city: '**there will be a plaza... where the governor's house will be built. Starting from this plaza is the single street that will go around four times: first in two circuits that will have a spiral shape and afterwards followed by two more with an octagonal shape... All doors and windows face the inside of the fortress, making the backs of the houses a continuous wall. The last row of houses will lean against the city ramparts thereby forming a gigantic snail.**'[54]

The spiral routes will surprise invaders: '**even if the enemy were to seize part of it, the central nucleus will always be free.**' Bernard Palissy called the shell-houses cabinets. '**The façade of the cabinet will be built with unpolished, uncut stones, so that the façade will not have the shape of a building**', unlike the inside which must be as smooth as the inside of a shell. Gaston Bachelard adds: '**He wants the wall that protects his very being to be smooth, polished, and hermetic, as though his sensitive flesh were to touch the walls of the house. In Palissy's dream, the function of living can be interpreted as related to touch. The shell allows complete physical intimacy. The home inhabited by Palissy had the design characteristics of his twisted cabinet with several humps and oblique hollows without any appearance of art form, sculpture, or man-made work. The vaults with several hanging humps give one the feeling that they are about to fall. The inside of the house is bathed in enamel; the outside is covered with dirt that is sown with plants and trees. Everything happens in a spiral buried in the rocks formed by man, in the image and likeness of the work of nature.**'

**Figure 1.73**
(a and b)
Guggenheim
Museum in New
York, USA. Frank
Lloyd Wright,
1956. A fine
example of
continuity of
space, structure
and shape. ©
International
Stock.

(a)

(b)

By way of conclusion to these comments and
thoughts about molluscs, particularly Gastropods,
here, once again, are some words by Wright:

*If you really want to study building, nature is the best place to do it... Observe the innate capacity for invention revealed in these minute residences built by hundreds of small, natural creatures. Each one has built his house with a lovely, unmistakable variation that never ends... If you want a lesson in organic structure where what we call ornamentation is an appropriate sequence and the consequence of shape and method, here you have it. What marvellous construction! What beautiful texture and what admirable colour! These natural houses are small poems... None of them ever ceases to express its beginning, that which gave them birth and governs all births.*[55]

# HUMANITY: OUR SPACE THROUGH THE AGES

02

*... And it appears that with a transformation and the acquisition of vitality, intelligence, and courage, he leaves the caverns to confront the wild beasts and decide who will govern the face of the earth.*

Alfonso Olvera Lôpez

## Vernacular architecture

Just as the history of music has concentrated on great classical music while virtually ignoring popular music and the history of literature has concentrated on ancient and modern classics while virtually ignoring the oral tradition, so the history of architecture has concentrated on magnificent structures and virtually ignored the important contribution made by vernacular architecture.

Small, anonymous dwellings constructed to provide a home and shelter can be found in virtually any human settlement. This special style of architecture is called, among other things, rural, indigenous, anonymous, or vernacular, architecture. Vernacular architecture has survived thanks to knowledge being passed down from one generation to another; it is a type of traditional architecture. Those who live in it build their own homes with the help of the community. Although one of the most essential characteristics of vernacular architecture is that it is not normally the work of professionals, another

> Back in those times when the truth was confused with mythology, we see a creature running from inclement weather and from pre-historic beasts which pursue him because of his insignificant physical size. It seems he is destined to become the next meal of the beasts that stalk him. Seized with fear, he flees to hide his weakness in the caverns that nature has placed within his reach. And it appears that with a transformation and the acquisition of vitality, intelligence, and courage, he leaves the caverns to confront the wild beasts and decide who will govern the face of the earth
>
> Alfonso Olvera López[2]

important element is that the buildings are in keeping with their geographical surroundings, traditions and culture. The architect Tadeus Torucki, for example, wrote an article entitled 'Man's Dwelling' in which he referred to the city of Las Vegas, where many buildings are not built by professionals but still cannot, he argued, be classified as vernacular because they are completely foreign to their environment.[2] In the lost cities that rise up in the so-called poverty belts of large cities, the homes do not represent vernacular architecture for the same reason.

Since vernacular architecture depends directly on its geographical surroundings, it's almost as if it's a natural product. It establishes complete symbiosis with the local ecosystem and it economises on raw materials and energy. With vernacular architecture, natural materials are used and tools provided locally so that a semi-industrial process is not needed. The shapes and forms used derive from well-defined needs, so they blend into the local landscape. Here, humans do not impose – they adjust. Those building today apply the empirical knowledge of their ancestors, though they learn from the mistakes of the past and add to the knowledge as new needs arise.

Vernacular architecture reflects what people and their relationships are like. In vernacular populations each new integrated home enriches all the rest. Generally, like a good wine, the older these villages are, the more worthy they are of esteem.

Vernacular architecture also maintains the individuality of its creators. In spite of meeting the same basic needs, using local materials and, even more importantly, using empirical knowledge from the same sources, each home is individual and the dwellings of one village, although similar, are distinct from those of a neighbouring village. This is why professional architects are increasingly paying more attention to it. This interest really began with the exhibition called 'Architecture without Architects', shown in the Museum of Modern Art, New York City, in 1964.

Vernacular architecture is an example of how often simple answers to the problems of physical surroundings produce very satisfactory results. Simple answers are the more functional but often, paradoxically, they are the most complex to achieve.

We will now examine the intimate relationship between nature and humans, and how it can be applied to our designs. The transition of the vernacular to the contemporary is known as extrapolated architecture.

The general belief is that humans evolved as erect-walking hominids on earth more than 3,500,000 years ago (Johanson and Edey, 1981; 1990). For a long time, they survived by gathering food and seeking refuge in their natural environment. They did not change anything; they merely adapted to it. The physical world was the realm of nature; its antonym, culture, was just beginning to manifest the first signs of existence. During most of this time, human groups slept in trees to protect themselves from animal attacks.

The lifestyle of sedentary humans is very recent. The Palaeolithic Age, the age of the nomadic, accounts for more than 95 per cent of the total time-span of the human race.

### The Refuge of Neanderthal Man

Neanderthal Man appeared in Europe 100,000 or
more years ago. Until about 40,000 BC we
imagine him with a beard, a prominent jawbone,
and coarse, uncouth movements, living in a cave.
Instead we should regard him as an extremely
ingenious being who knew how to adapt to the
climate and his immediate environment. We
must bear in mind that most inventions were still
far in the future. A more common term for
Neanderthal Man is caveman because he used
caves for shelter. Although natural formations,
they were chosen very carefully. Firstly, the cave
opening had to be south facing, away from the
cold, arctic winds which came from the north.
Secondly, there had to be sufficient airflow for the
fire, which was kept in a rather large but not
very deep hole and played an extremely
important role in the functioning of the cave.
Ventilation could be increased by making a rut
that conducted air from the mouth of the cave to
the flames in the centre, encouraging
combustion. Mammoth bones cut into small
pieces, manure, and evergreen branches were
used as fuel.

**Figure 2.1**
The cave was a vital
space for
Neanderthal Man.

Several families could enjoy warmth and
camaraderie inside the cave. Winter limited the
number of hunting and gathering trips that could
be made, and the families spent most of their time
in the cave. While men went out to look for wild,
edible plants, the women carried out domestic
duties, cooking the food or caring for the
children. They had a varied diet low in salt and
sugar – except for the honey they occasionally
found – and high in fibre. The meat they ate was
very low in fat because it came from wild animals
that had 70% less fat than the domesticated ones
we now have. Water was their main drink.

Fire was invaluable during this period, not
only as a tool for life – to cook food, keep warm,
provide light and keep wild animals away – but
also as something which encouraged humans to
live together in peace. The centre of community
life (and of the cave) was the fire around which
everyone gathered. As time passed, the fire
became a fireplace that was still later substituted
by a television. Nowadays many bedrooms have
their own television, contributing to the further
disintegration of the family.

The cave was our first shelter, the first place
we felt that we both owned and were part of.
This safe place, where difficulties with humidity
and a lack of natural light were gradually solved
over time, was also where the history of
architecture begins and develops, to the point
that we sought and created new shapes and
methods for building shelters. The cave gave us
housing and tranquillity at the same time. To put
this into perspective, we should remember the
words of the Latin American storyteller, Horacio
Quiroga: '...**when the men were convinced that
the beast would not enter, and the cave was
consequently unassailable, the growls of the
animal were met with flying stones and loud
yells. Housing and peaceful sleep had been
conquered forever.**'[3]

## The refuge of Cro-Magnon Man

The next evolutionary link also appeared in Europe approximately 40,000 years ago: Cro-Magnon Man. Cultural development really started during this period.

Behind his savage appearance, Cro-Magnon Man turned out to be intelligent, intrepid, mystic, innovative, and artistic. He was the first to use 'spare time' creatively – which is indispensable for cultural development. With Cro-Magnon man, the age of the nomadic hunter ended, and the agricultural age of sedentary life began.

The accidental discovery of ruins in Les Eyzies, France, in 1968 revealed a typical Cro-Magnon landscape. The road workers who found this settlement could not have imagined how important it was. It's as if the geology had been designed for man to live in. The complicated valleys are like wide boulevards that made communication between inhabitants possible as they moved between the cliffs and through the caves. Within these rocky masses, shaped more than 100 million years ago, lived Cro-Magnon Man.

Although Neanderthal Man had already developed objects such as tools from nature, Cro-Magnon Man used more skill and dexterity when making his utensils. Each one was different as the craftsman carved out bone, stone, or horn in such a way as to take advantage of its natural shape and texture. It is very probable that Cro-Magnon Man invented the technique of working gold or silver by fire. He also became more interested in his clothing, covering himself with animal skins and making different kinds of clothes suitable for different conditions – it was Cro-Magnon Man who initiated the great migrations to the Arctic regions.

The animal kingdom provided Cro-Magnon Man with meat for food, skins for clothes, and bones for tools. The vegetable kingdom provided food, clothing, and tools: he ate fruit, covered himself with branches, and used wild roots for tools. The mineral kingdom provided refuge and the raw materials for most of his tools.

Especially important was his art. When the frescos in caves at Altamira, Spain were finally dated, Cro-Magnon Man was recognised as the first artist. Walter Benjamin held that art is what humanises us. Perhaps it is an extreme opinion, but he thought that the history of humanity could not be construed without art history. The origins of art can be found in our practical needs.

There are plenty of examples: at some moment of pre-history, a hunter disguised himself as an animal in order to lure his prey; another conceived the idea of synchronising communal work by singing some rhythmical song; still another individualised his tool by engraving a distinct ornament on it.

The emergence of art meant that Palaeolithic Man started to view the world in a different way. While trying to explain the world around him, he invented magic, and art immediately became his most faithful instrument. Ernest Fischer explains this in very few words: '**Reality was converted to myth, the magic ceremony was converted to art.**'[4]

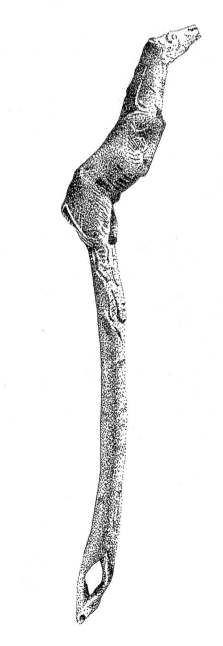

**Figure 2.2**
A horse rearing on its hind legs carved in a reindeer's antler. Its aerodynamic shape is suggested by the antler itself. Bruniquel, France, 13,000 BC.

Art fulfilled a specific social function. Artists could explain something to the world; for instance they interpreted a thunderbolt, deciphered natural cycles, and gave meaning to earthquakes and droughts. As a result the artist must have made the world a more habitable place, hence the relationship was born between art and dwellings. Cro-Magnon Man never framed nor signed his art because it was always part of his surroundings. Through his works of art, he looked for harmony with Nature both for himself and for others like him.

The caves at Altamira are a series of winding tunnels, crevices, and chambers that were slowly sculpted over millions of years by rainwater penetrating the rocks and moulding the sediments.

*Imagine this: in these dark, silent caves, small shimmers of light can be seen coming from one chamber. The light comes from a weak flame in a rustic lantern on a rock. In the middle of this subtle splendour stands a man with long hair, dressed in skins and wearing a shell necklace, completely absorbed in painting. Most of his colours have been obtained from soft rocks in red, orange, yellow and brown tones, to which animal fat or blood has been added. He has placed these in large shells or hollow bones and then ground and mixed them together until he has achieved a thick, pasty paint. Now he soaks a piece of leather in the paint, removes it impregnated with colour, and smears it on the rock jutting out above him. The painting begins to take on a three-dimensional quality that integrates with the cave itself, and little by little the picture emerges from the wall, blending with both rock and cave: Arsculpain – architecture, sculpture, and painting – become an organic whole.*

Within the cave dwellings of Cro-Magnon Man, organic architecture makes its debut.

## Troglodyte architecture

The cave can be considered to be the starting point for the history of architecture; it was our first shelter. However, caves are natural formations and primitive humans made very few modifications to them. The transformation process really began with troglodyte architecture.

A cave was used mostly as a lair rather than as a home. Humans occupied caves principally in winter or during adverse weather conditions. The appearance of the 'house' as a daily habitat came later with agricultural development and the domestication of animals. Troglodyte architecture was the first answer to the problem of the dwelling within the new parameters of sedentary life. This was determined by the social organisation of agricultural work. The troglodyte habitat was made up of a group of 'houses'; it was community architecture. These houses were below the earth, taking advantage of natural cavities or being dug by the inhabitants. With troglodyte architecture, humans began to create, transform and alter their physical surroundings in order to increase well-being, establishing a real symbiotic relationship with the environment.

It is easy to see why humans developed the buried home. Firstly, there was the climatic factor: troglodyte constructions provided a wonderful answer in regions with extreme weather conditions because the thermal (earth) masses make it is easier to maintain a relatively constant temperature. Secondly, strategically speaking, the subterranean dwelling ensured excellent shelter – a human's reasons for living underground were similar to those of animals such as ants, moles, rabbits, and so on. Finally, there were structural and religious reasons.

Bernard Rudofsky thinks that the clearest and most imposing model of troglodyte architecture is the dwellings used by old colonies of monks and nuns in Cappadocia in the mountains of Turkey.[5] This landscape was produced by eruptions from two volcanoes. When the lava hardened, it formed a porous stone

**Figure 2.3**
Artist's impression of Cro-Magnon Man smearing paint on a projecting rock in the Altamira caves in Spain. (c)Aldi Oyarsabal.

**Figure 2.4**
The porous stone tufa, of Cappadocia, Turkey eroded by wind and water. Monks and nuns made these 'caves' their home.

called tufa. As the years passed, the wind and water eroded the tufa, creating fantastic shapes. At the beginning of the eighth century AD, when the colony in Cappadocia was first being chiselled out of the earth, the Arabs were already moving westwards, so the Christian monks and nuns sought protection during the Holy War, hiding below the surface and sculpting what Rudofsky himself called earth-scrapers. In Derinkuyo and Raymakli, for example, these earth-scrapers reached as far down as ten levels below the surface.

The salt mine at Weiliczka in what is now Poland sheltered a city formed by pillars, arches, and vaults of hard calcareous rock as bright and shiny as crystal. There is a labyrinth of tunnels around 100 kilometres long and 30 metres deep.

**Figure 2.5**
A rural community in China excavated in soft soil.

In northern China, particularly in the provinces of Shensi, Shansi, Kansu, and Honan, dwellings for whole communities have been built underground. There is a lack of cultivable land for agriculture so what there is, is dedicated solely to farming, and the peasants have excavated their homes. Villages go unnoticed, except for the fact that you can see smoke rising out of the fields and, if you approach, chimneys, open patios and ladders. The open patios are of great importance here because sunlight cannot, for all practical purposes, enter the underground compound that enjoys constant cool temperatures; the people, therefore, cook, eat, work, and collect water in cisterns on these patios.

There is still some underground construction today. One example is on the Côte D'Azur, France, where the high cost of land is a determining factor. A deep shaft is generally dug, which functions as the centre of the project.

Imagine whole underground cities: factories, shops, cinemas, offices, public buildings, housing... If we stop to think about the alarming demographical and ecological problems we currently face, these cities become not only an architectural curiosity but also probably the most viable solution to the future problem of housing. Another advantage with this type of construction is that it does not interfere with the scenery.

## The mobile dwelling

Although the building of the first housing came with the development of agriculture, a very important historical period existed between this new life and the old routine of the hunter–gatherer: the great migrations. Humans had to use their wits to find a safe, warm, dry place to spend the night during long journeys. As time passed, groups of nomads who followed the animals they were hunting were also confronted with the problems of finding shelter.

In the middle of unlimited natural space, it was necessary to create a closed, limited space for shelver: a portable dwelling. The tent appeared under these circumstances. The tent is, at least in evolutionary if not necessarily in chronological terms, an intermediate stage between natural shelters and the first distinctly human constructions.

**Figure 2.6**
Prototypes of mobile housing. The Neanderthal protection, constructed basically with animal skins and mammoth bones, 44,000 years old, and the tent, 13,000 years old, are both found in the same region of the Ukraine.

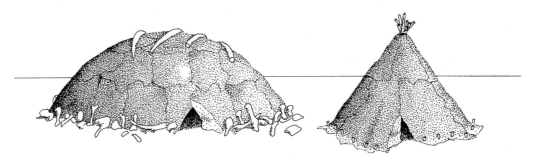

**Figure 2.7**
An example of a tent dwelling constructed with natural materials like underbrush and dry branches.

The tent is one of the oldest artefacts which is still useful in the modern world; it is one of the most ingenious shelters humans have produced. Today, nomadic tribes use tents extensively in areas where natural shelters are scarce, such as the tundra, desert, steppe, prairie, unobstructed space and flat terrain.

A painstaking process was involved in making the tent what it is today. Every time a nomadic tribe set up and dismantled their camp, they tried to think how they could make the work easier and quicker. They also wanted materials and shapes that would weigh less and be easier to handle. This resulted in the tent – a portable dwelling that was very light and easy to put up and take down.

The tent has been used in every part of the world, and although the methods and construction materials might vary, the basic principal is almost the same in every case: a membrane is stretched as tightly as possible over a light frame. The frame was originally a wooden structure, circular or oval at the base. The membrane supports a tensile stress while the frame receives the pressure stress. The supporting elements, when united at the top, take on a conical or dome-like shape. Generally, the position of a tent is determined beforehand by the orientation of the entrance.

Tent coverings have evolved. Initially, they were natural materials like underbrush, dry branches, palm leaves, and skins. Later they became woven materials and finally synthetic fibres. These modifications have helped lighten the weight, provide greater resistance to wind and rain, and attain greater durability and pliability.

The most primitive nomadic group in Europe, the Laplanders in what is today Norway, probably used the tent mainly in summer when they moved their herds to fresh grazing lands. Their tents were covered with animal skins.

The North American Indians built their tents with rudimentary tools. They used sharp stones to carve the tips of long sticks over which they fastened animal skins, creating a conical structure that was very strong and easy to move.

The tents of the Tartars from Siberia and Mongolia have dome-like shapes. The frames are constructed from reeds put together with pivots, making it easier to spread the tents out in a single movement like giant umbrellas. In these areas, tents give protection primarily from wind and sand.

In Africa there are abundant examples of transient dwellings. In West Africa tents are like cabins built with flexible and resistant green sticks, covered with strips of grass and palm. Two people can set up these cabins in a few hours. There is a small entrance to crawl through. During cold weather a fire can be built in a hole in the centre of the cabin. For sleeping, a hole is sculpted out of the earth, in the shape of a person, or a skin is laid out.

**Figure 2.8**
Bedouin tents provide a solution to the problems posed by location and resources. © Sue Roaf.

The tents of the Zulus in Southern Africa are built with green sticks, but in the shape of arches so that they resemble a giant beehive covered with straw. They also differ in that when the Zulus move on they leave the tents, as they know that wherever they next stop they will find the necessary materials to be able to make them again. What is portable, therefore, is not the dwelling itself but the concept of the dwelling.

The German architect and engineer Frei Otto estimates that 20–50 million people live in tents today.[6] In Arabia alone there are whole tented cities with up to two million inhabitants. The portable dwelling, an evolutionary bridge between the nomad and the farmer and direct ancestor of the prefabricated house, still has things to teach us: its simplicity and usefulness; its short-lived nature in one location; its continuous use.

Floating houses and houses on wheels or sliding like sleighs, have added a touch of adventure to the mobile dwelling of the past.

### The first builders

In the first built structures, humans followed the example of animals. They built with earth, mud, stone, and vegetable fibres – the materials at their fingertips. Archaeological remains indicate that the first constructions appeared about 12,000 years ago. Neanderthals took refuge in a cave; the troglodytes continued under the cover of rock; but the first constructors built. Building implies a conscious, deliberate use of tools as an extension of a human's motor capacity as well as an idea of what it is they wish to build. When humans built for the first time, the face of the Earth changed.

The first constructions imitated natural shapes. Initially, they were semi-underground. When humans found a crack in the ground, they took advantage of the natural covering of a fallen tree and ingeniously created a dwelling. They put dirt along the edge of cracks and moulded it into the correct shape. The house grew depending how they inserted the soil.

The Neolithic village of Lindenthal, Germany, is representative of this type of architecture. It has been extremely difficult to make a model of it because there are no ruins left, only cavities and even then the original appearance of these cavities has been obscured by numerous studies, both archaeological and architectural. Lindenthal, colony and shelter of a whole Neolithic community, was a group of integrated houses, yet each was original, in spite of having been built by a people with similar needs and identical means. The backbone of their architecture, free design, made it possible for inhabitants to give their own dwelling a touch of individuality. There is very obvious harmony between the group and the ecosystem. Lindenthal can be seen as a junction between troglodyte architecture, the mobile dwelling, and the first constructions.

*Every architect at some time in his life should make a house with his own hands. Feeling the materials in his hands and hearing the voices of spaces demanding their existence will give him time to be daring and humble*

Richard England[7]

**Figure 2.9**
Origins of the first
constructions.

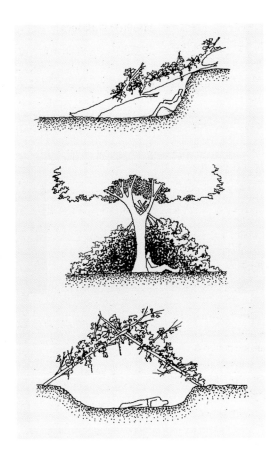

The dwellings at Lindenthal provided ample
space for both physical and emotional comfort.
There were numerous curved lines: anonymous
Neolithic architects favoured free forms and for
that reason dedicated time and labour to
sculpting the inside of their homes. Rudofsky
talks about sculptural ground, modelled out of
hollows, which invite one to lie down and enjoy
the space, just functional enough to be useful.
With so-called 'progress', humans have lost
tactile contact with their environment. I agree
with Rudofsky: '**The more one observes the
reconstruction of a Lindenthal house, the
more one doubts it should be called
primitive....**'[8]

Wherever buildings have appeared, in
whatever climate, at whatever altitude, clever use
of the raw materials that the environment has
provided has been made. Ice, skins, clay, wood,
leaves, stone, mud, dirt: the result depends on the
wit, inventiveness, creativity and intelligence of
the builder. There is nowhere in the world where
it is not possible to create some kind of dwelling.

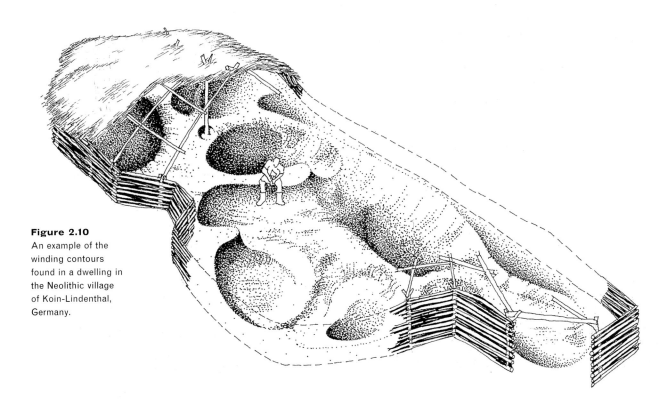

**Figure 2.10**
An example of the
winding contours
found in a dwelling in
the Neolithic village
of Koin-Lindenthal,
Germany.

Nowadays, the invention of artificial climate through air-conditioning systems and heaters has meant that the materials and designs for homes are similar whatever their location. For thousands of years, the type of dwelling built depended directly on the climate. If we want to stop abusing our energy resources, we need to return to vernacular techniques.

Vernacular constructions have solved climatic problems in regions with extreme temperatures. Architectural styles vary from one place to another. In deserts where there is little rainfall, flat roofs are the norm, while in rainy areas sloped roofs are used. The size of windows varies according to sunshine, view, required ventilation and personal inclination.

In some places there are only two seasons: the rainy season and the dry, hot season. In Nigeria, homes have a double dome – a rounded clay shell that gives form to the soffit inside equipped with protruding wooden stakes supporting another roof made of straw. This roof is like an umbrella in the rainy season while the hay absorbs the heat during the dry season. The air cushion between the roofs provides general insulation.

On this planet, four basic climatic zones can be distinguished: the Arctic region, the open prairies, the desert, and the jungles/forests. In each of these, homes have been designed and built.

### The arctic region

The Arctic region is characterised by constantly low temperatures, icy winds, and a weak sun that barely gives light during the winter. The whiteness of the scenery is almost absolute and the risk of going blind very real. Without visual references, as anthropologist Robert Flaherty described: **'there is no middle distance nor perspective nor silhouette nor anything else that can stick to one's visual memory except thousands of wispy snow flurries running along the ground before the wind. It is a land without boundaries, and it has no end.'**[9] Here, there are inadequate adjectives to describe the cold. It is difficult to move over the snow and gusts of wind blow like razor blades cutting the air.

This inhospitable region is inhabited by the Eskimos, an ethnic group with Mongolian features and possible Mongol origins. They live in igloos, perhaps the most interesting and efficient of all invented shelters. The environment has forced them to live a semi-nomadic culture. Winter is a bonanza during which the whole family undertakes hunting and fishing trips.

The construction of an igloo is steeped in ritual related to the Eskimo's life of hunting. The place where the first seal is caught determines the exact place where the igloo will be built. From there the Eskimo looks for the flattest surface he can find with the hardest snow and draws a circle here, the radius of which is equal to his own height. With the sole help of a walrus bone used as a knife, the Eskimo cuts blocks of ice approximately 90 centimetres long, 45 centimetres wide, and 15 centimetres deep. He pulls these blocks of ice out of the surface in such a way that he performs two tasks at the same time: excavating and building.

There are two basic methods for the construction of an igloo. The first consists of placing the blocks in such a way that they form concentric rings. Each ring decreases in diameter as the igloo rises until it is completely sealed off at the dome-like top. The second method consists of placing the blocks of ice next to each other raising them in an ascending spiral shape. This method begins by placing the first three pieces of ice at a slant to lead to the formation of the dome. The igloo is made from the inside, slanting it slightly towards the centre. Finally the last block of ice is put in place at the top of the dome, as high as the Eskimo with his arms stretched upwards. The Eskimo does not require a measuring stick – he simply uses his body to build his home to his own scale, as do other animals in this region.

**Figure 2.11**
An igloo: method of construction.

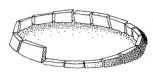

The last piece of ice placed in the upper part of the igloo is generally transparent, serving as a window to give natural light. These crystallised blocks are hard to find, so it is not uncommon to see Eskimos transporting them for weeks on their sleds. Once the blocks of ice are in place, cracks and crannies are filled with loose ice from the outside. Then the wind takes charge, solidifying the whole structure.

Once the outside of the igloo has been built, the woman's work begins. The first thing she does is to cover the opening with skins. She then lights a lamp which uses seal or whale blubber. This produces heat, but it is also the beginning of a very interesting process inside the igloo. The humidity evaporates and raises the temperature to that of dew, and the condensation produced soaks the inside of the walls. The drops of water do not fall; instead they start running down the igloo's curved walls. Once the walls are completely wet, the skins are removed from the opening and the icy wind that enters freezes the water covering the walls, thereby creating a coat of ice that plugs up the seams. This solidifies the igloo resulting in an almost monolithic construction. It also prevents the warm air inside leaving and the cold air outside entering. In short, the igloo is like an insulated, thermal dome.

The usual entrance to an igloo is through a passage dug beneath the snow. This has two advantages: it prevents the loss of warm air that tends to rise, and keeps the cold arctic wind from penetrating. The tunnel is just high enough for a woman crouching with a baby on her back to get in – but too small for a polar bear. The entrance points away from the prevailing wind. The final result is a wonder of human ingenuity. The average temperature inside an igloo stays at a more or less constant 15° Celsius, while the outside temperature is 40° Celcius below zero.

Thermal stability is achieved because of the heat of the lanterns and body heat; the entrance tunnel controls the ventilation.

Inside a platform of snow covered with bear skins serves as the family's bed. This snow bed is placed approximately 70 centimetres above the ground to take advantage of the warm air that rises. The rest of the ground is covered with sealskins. The provisions, the sled and the dogs stay in the access tunnel. Within a relatively small space, the igloo has everything a family strictly needs: they can cook, eat, rest and sleep in it and it is warm and safe. When the season changes, the igloo is abandoned and eventually melts.

The admirable service that the igloo provides is due to its shape and the material used. The hemispheric dome has maximum resistance to the wind because of the exposure of a minimum part of its surface. It has probably taken about 10,000 years for the structure and the basic method of construction to evolve. This efficient and inventive system of construction (economy, simplicity, rapidity) has enabled the Eskimo to obtain a balanced whole in harmony with his environment.

Since the first expeditions people have had a great impact on the Arctic. Starting with the discoveries of huge quantities of oil reserves in Alaska, oil companies have modified the surroundings in such a violent way that the Eskimo culture could very well disappear before being fully understood. At the present time many Eskimo communities in Canada and Alaska have suffered a series of changes caused by incoming foreigners. Little by little they have stopped building igloos, substituting them with wooden houses or plastic igloos that are not always efficient. The snowmobile has, in the same way, replaced sleds pulled by dogs.

**Figure 2.12**
Cross-section of an igloo.

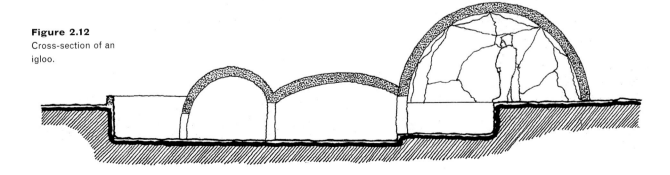

### The desert

During the day the desert reflects the sun's rays in every direction; there is a general absence of shadows in the blinding light. The wind penetrates space and moulds the topography into short-lived sand dunes and hyperactive sand. At night the cold seizes control of the desert with freezing gusts of wind. Anyone living here needs to be able to insulate themselves from heat during the day and conserve this heat for the cold night in an area where there are almost no rocks or trees with which to make a shelter.

In earlier times, the human dug a home under the ground where they could find water and protection against sandstorms and the heat. Later, they used the earth itself as a building material. The good, sandy clay and firm turf is moistened, kneaded and then mixed with manure or a fibrous plant-like straw to give it greater strength. In the beginning this mixture was moulded by hand into balls. Later, the walls were built of adobe, a Spanish word meaning sun-dried clay.

The Dogones, who live in north-eastern Africa, build in this way. They have settled on the edges of arid zones in the middle of cultivated areas. The components of their settlements possess admirable morphological and symbolic wealth. Colours and textures fit together well. The huts built of earth and straw, and the colour of the locals' skin and hair, blend and change with the colours of the landscape, which range from ochre to maroon. Everything reflects and is associated with the environment.

The shapes of the community are characterised by the curves of bodies, dwellings, utensils, animals and landscape. From an aerial viewpoint the village is anthropomorphic as are all its sections. Everything is contained in an oval-shaped area the centre of which is allotted to the cattle; the whole resembles a placenta.

Some villages have a dozen cylinder-shaped huts designated for the head of the family, the women, the children, the kitchen, granaries and workshops. The household furniture and effects are modest: earthen and wooden bowls, leather sacks for lard, skins to keep milk in, ostrich eggshells for drinking water, weapons, and so on.

**Figure 2.13**
A Dogon leaving his hut surrounded by different tones of ochre. © Image State.

**Figure 2.14**
(a) Layout of a
Dhordo village; (b)
Sketch of a Dhordo
home.

The cylindrical shape of the dwelling is well-suited to a region exposed to wind. Besides being easy to shield, this shape makes it possible to position the huts in such a way as to leave room for a large patio in the middle. The patio is the main area for family gatherings during the dry season and assumes the role of kitchen, workshop, and corral for domestic animals.

Married couples build homes with the aid of relatives and friends as part of a ritual. The dirt is taken out by hand, a stone foundation is placed over the ground, and then adobe bricks or earthen balls are laid in place, alternating the joints to avoid fissures. To create these austere mud huts, the people turn to a ceremony where matter and spirit join together using an artistic language while they mould and sculpt the earth. Thus they express their deepest, creative impulses and reflect their personalities in a great variety of visual and tactile shapes. The roof is made on the ground with branches, becoming light armour-shaped like a cone; this 'hat' is laid on top of branches which protrude from the sides of the house to keep water away from the walls. The cornice of branches also works as a scaffold for repairs. Then the structure is covered with layers of interwoven hay that make it very wind-resistant. Finally, the tip of the roof is tied with rope and covered with an earthen pot to guarantee a perfect, airtight seal.

Sculptural architecture in certain African and Middle Eastern cultures reaches its zenith with sensual forms similar to erotic art. For these cultures, soil is the most fertile element on earth and a strong symbol of sexuality, and they apply it as decoration with great and variable vitality. Contemplating these huts evokes a very special feeling: the fertility of the earth, represented by the naturalness of curvaceous lines, inspires pleasure. The craftsmen of Mali find intense delight in being able to make use of this material.

The huts are changed little by little as needs arise. Men and women live out a playful ritual that makes it possible for them to remake, reinterpret and revitalise them every year after the rainy season. In order to achieve this, building becomes an act of pleasure that does not require any complex technology or academic knowledge. They begin with a decision made by each individual to unite himself harmoniously with the inherited culture and with the spirit of the place. One of the perennial charms of this architecture is that it avoids uniformity. Von Wutenau said it very well: '**The imperfect with grace is better than the perfect without grace.**'[10]

In the Middle East there are cities that were founded centuries ago. Remains of buildings made with dirt have been found dating back 12,000 years. The Tower of Babel was built with clay approximately 27,000 years ago. Chanchan, 570 kilometres from Lima, Peru, and dating from around 1000 AD, is the largest clay city in the world; although the original constructions are presently uninhabited, the local villagers still use adobe houses. The original process changed with the invention of moulds; it takes only two weeks in the blazing sun for the blocks to solidify.

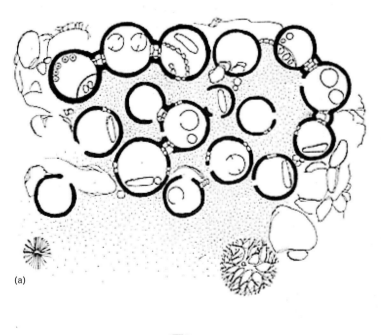

(a)

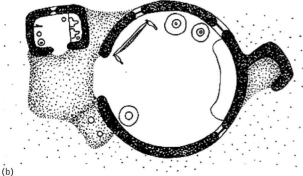

(b)

**Figure 2.15**
An example of constructions made with adobe.

**Figure 2.16**
The mosque at Djenne, Mali. © Photo Researchers, Inc.

Homes made with a material like adobe are extremely efficient in desert climates. The clay absorbs the burning rays of the sun throughout the day, but its solidity prevents the heat from penetrating inside. Later, when night has fallen, the adobe bricks radiate the stored heat. Not only are adobe bricks functional, they are naturally inexpensive.

At the present time in Lima, Peru, the four million inhabitants who live in marginalised areas have rejected adobe as a construction material. Their dream is to build a two-storey house with partitions, made of iron and reinforced concrete with a roof of asbestos and gold-coloured aluminium. On weekends, thousands of families choose to build homes like these. '**Socially speaking, adobe is considered inferior. It symbolises backwardness**', points out architect Manuel Ungaro.[11] Paradoxically, some of the smartest mansions in the north western part of the United States are being built with adobe.

Thirty years ago, two-thirds of the world's population lived in homes made with earth; now only one-third does. Owings, an American architect and co-founder of the largest architectural offices in the world (Skidmore, Owings and Merrill) and considered *the* epitome of the so-called 'international style', chose to build his house with adobe because: '**This house is built with natural materials. You can build a perfectly good house with adobe without using any metal at all. I tend to oppose the mechanical aspects of modern times.**'[12]

For the populated areas around the Mediterranean Sea, painting with lime constitutes a fundamental, satisfying ritual. Lime is a make-up that covers defects and acquires its hardness through the application of multiple coats, as with lacquer or mother-of-pearl. On some Mediterranean islands, E. Bradford writes: '**the floors are painted with lime twice a day. It is difficult to describe an atmosphere of such cleanliness except to say that one looks at the bottom of his shoes before stepping out on to the main street.**'[13] The arrangement of the houses is rhythmical and expresses the characteristics of the topography. The dwellings are interconnected with each other by means of steps that skirt the natural slope of the property. The width, height and depth of the steps are modified fortuitously causing surprise which, according to Rudofsky: '**disconcerts whoever has been accustomed to walking mechanically all his life.**'[14]

**Figure 2.17**
A house in
Tlacotalpan,
Veracruz, Mexico.

The Mexican peasant concentrates on just one space that satisfies his basic needs: protection, storage and intimacy. He owns a little simple furniture – a straw sleeping mat on the floor which is rolled up during the day – and trunks or baskets in which he can put clothing and other important objects when they're not being used. He has nothing superfluous. The outlying fields and the patios are created in an atmosphere of work, conversation, rest and celebration. In the streets, which are made of soft packed dirt, or along the grassy paths, people talk to each other, watch and find peace. Today, however, some of these areas are condemned to chaos. The peasant watches his space being invaded by outside influences that destroy his architectural culture, substituting traditional materials with others.

For buildings to be in harmony with the landscape, they need prolonged contact with nature. It could be said that exposure to sun, wind and rain produces a patina that affects them with time. The shape is born out of a combination of the constructor's tradition and the essence of life.

## Jungle regions

Vernacular buildings in the jungle try, generally successfully, to give protection from the rain, the

**Figure 2.18**
In a detail of a blue wall of the house (photo at left), the paint has been transformed by the sun, wind and rain, creating a patina that has been there for some time. © Alejandro Martinez Mena.

**Figure 2.19**
An example of the type of hut commonly found in jungle regions.

heat and savage beasts. Plants provide the raw materials. Branches or trunks, including bamboo and ditch reeds, are used for the frame. The roof is made with leaves, palm branches, grass and straw. These materials are immediately available, easy to handle, enormously resistant to water and they're strong. The shape is determined by climatic conditions: the roof must have a steep enough slope to allow rainwater to drain quickly during storms. The roof hangs down below the walls to protect the dwelling from rain, sun and wind.

In order to attain good ventilation, walls are built with interwoven ditch reeds and leaves that, in some cases, may be rolled up during the day. In addition to this, some dwellings are built above ground-level to improve ventilation and give protection from floods. Inside, built-in furniture is arranged in such a way as to leave the centre of the home free, thereby encouraging cross-ventilation.

Examples abound. Wherever we find vernacular buildings, we find a deep knowledge of the physical surroundings and harmony with the landscape. The value of this vernacular architecture rests in the way that, without offending physical surroundings, it manages to give personality to its craft.

## Arches, vaults and domes

The basic idea sustained in the great structures of every period has been to cover large clearings with minimal material and maximum efficiency. Designers found models for this in nature, represented in curved structural surfaces, which inspired them to build arches, vaults and domes. The arch was born of a vital understanding of the coverings of plants and animals and was constructed like ribs in a network of branches or in the tangled disorder of a wing or flipper.

**Figure 2.20**
An arch formed by the forces of nature.

❝Not only did the arch give its name to architecture, it also beautified it ❞

Anonymous

**Figure 2.21**
Cross-section and
floor plan of the
Treasure of Atreus,
Mycenae, fourteenth
century BC.

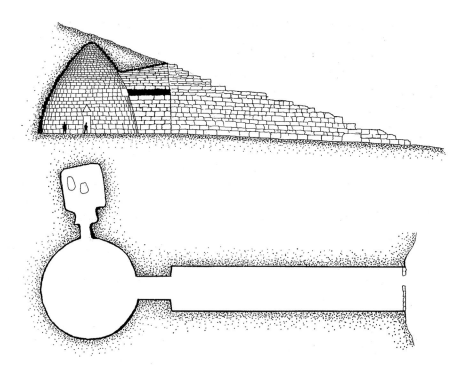

The arch represents a victory of the human's will to dominate space over the problems of heavy material and the force of gravity. Following the contours of the human silhouette with rising energy, it projects its possibilities in the concepts of the vault and the dome. This curved structure became a dominant feature in the architecture of Roman, Byzantine, Romanesque, Gothic, Renaissance and baroque styles.

The stone arch came about with an application of the material to a rational way of working, in other words, compression: the arch overcomes the force of gravity through compression, turning two weaknesses into a strength when united through a central block called a keystone.

The series of arches in concentric rows that gradually close, curving upwards until they give way to a narrow orifice crowned by one outside stone, led to the creation of vaulted structures. Buildings like the nuragas of Cerdeña and the tolos, tombs in the shape of a beehive in the Cyclades Islands, are examples of this process. The building system of the tolos reached its climax in the tomb known as the Treasure of Atreus; the construction was partly buried and is covered with a dome that is close to 14 metres high and almost equal to its diameter – and a technical feat for its time.

The Sumerians and Chaldeans used vaults and domes made of adobe and brick taken from the muddy terrain of the delta formed by the Rivers Euphrates and Tigris. In an area where wood and stone are scarce, the ancient civilisation of Mesopotamia built edifices of compact mass. They built solid, terraced towers called ziggurats on embankments; to keep the temperature cool they were closed up with vaults that provided protection from sun and rain. Spiral ramps took one to the top of the tower that served as an astronomical observatory, sometimes reaching a height of more than 80 metres. The mythical Tower of Babel was, perhaps, nothing more than an enormous ziggurat. Mesopotamia, then, first gave birth to the tradition of eastern architecture which later spread around the Mediterranean Sea.

**Figure 2.22**
Lotus flower and
Egyptian capital.

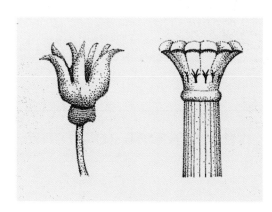

The Egyptian civilisation, which extended along the banks of the Nile River on the edge of the desert, used the fake vault of adobe and stone initially. The Egyptians later changed the way they built their funeral monuments and temples, centring the constructive axis in trapezoidal structures. The direct predecessors of the pyramids were the mastabas, tombs made of adobe or stone which had the shape of truncated pyramids and were modelled on a formal analogy of the pile of stones with which graves were covered in ancient times. The first tombs barely managed to keep the winds from blowing away the sand that covered the coffins.

The insides of the temples of the last Ancient Egyptian dynasties were built like oases of papyrus, lotus, and palms. The temple of Amon in Karnak has at least 314 columns and the ornamentation of the capitals, which recreate the shapes of the vegetation in the Nile Valley, are the result of a varied morphology.

Greek architecture, unlike Egyptian and Chaldean architecture found adjacent to their riverbanks, developed on the coasts of the Mediterranean. The gentle climate, like the beauty of the landscape, the light and the sky, made it possible for a great part of Grecian life to take place in the open air, which contributed to the health and strength of the race. This produced both a special character and an architecture in which outside spaces and sculptural volume were more important than inside spaces. In this sense, we can consider Greek architecture to be an expression of sculpture. Its buildings and temples were meant to be seen from the outside. Only priests were allowed inside the imposing Parthenon, for example, while the people were restricted to contemplating the exterior.

The shaft of each column was at first the trunk of a tree, with a geometrically adjusted shape. The function of the flutes was to regulate the trunk with the tools available at that time. The primitive function of the capital was to make a transition between the round shape of the columns and the shape of the abacus and the architrave; it also acted as a corbel by reducing the clearing of the top piece with its lateral projections. During the Renaissance period, when Greek architecture was being rediscovered, architects tried in vain to find the mathematical curve that the Greeks might have used for the Doric capital until they finally realised that no curve from analytic geometry had been used. Instead the Greeks had used the living shape of the sea urchin then so abundant in the Mediterranean. They found that the Ionic capital was based on the spiral, the result of marine motifs, while the Corinthian capital with its double acanthus leaves was inspired by stylised vegetation. The form of caryatids emulated the human body.

**Figure 2.23**
Sea urchin and archaic Greek capitals.

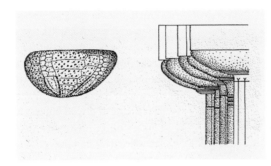

**Figure 2.24**
Classic orders: Doric, Ionic, and Corinthian capitals inspired by the sea urchin of the Mediterranean Sea, the mollusc and acanthus leaves, respectively.

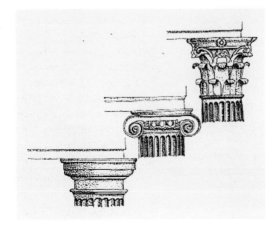

**Figure 2.25**
Trulli houses in
Apulia, Italy. Even
though no two
houses are the same,
the village has
managed to achieve
unity.

### Rome and the pantheon of Agrippa

Roman civilisation was characterised by its
complex urban areas, with their intricate,
monumental public buildings – thermal baths,
coliseums, the senate, the basilica,
commemorative arches – all placed along stone-
paved avenues with panoramic views, bridges,
and aqueducts.

The Roman concept of a building's interior
was basically rooted in a primitive, circular room
with added projections like an apse. This
technique of construction, imported from Greece,
Asia Minor, and Egypt, persists even to this day
in the trulli, houses with conical roofs that are
still built in Apulia, southern Italy. These
primitive, domed houses were the origins of the
monumental Roman edifices.

The word dome is derived from the Latin
word *domus*, which was primarily applied to a
shelter with a round roof. Later it would be
named the House of God – in Italian *duomo* and
in German *dom*. In his book *The Dome*, Professor
E. Baldwin Smith describes the dome as:

'**...hemisphere, beehive, onion, melon, and
bulb. In ancient times it was thought of as
Tholos, pine cone, the amalka tree, cosmic
egg, and celestial basin. As long as modern
terms are purely descriptive, the ancient ones
keep, at the same time, a certain
remembrance of the origin of the dome and
communicate something of the ancestral
beliefs regarding the supernatural meanings
associated with its shape.**'[15]

Immense arches and vaults made of concrete
were common on a large scale. The puzzolana (or
puzzolanic cement) made with light, porous rock
provided a material which, when mixed with
lime, produced a very adhesive, solid concrete.
The structural frame, composed of ribs and brick
arches, formed a constructive unity provided by
this mass of concrete. The walls, which supported
the heavy weight of the domes, are resistant and
were made practically and rapidly by pouring the
puzzolana into wooden moulds. Following this
procedure the Romans made their most daring
domes and vaults: ringed roofs or barrel vaults;
groined vaults, formed by the intersection of two
barrel vaults in open spaces; penetration vaults
and the great spherical domes.

The most representative example of a
spherical dome is, without doubt, Agrippa's
Pantheon, built by Emperor Hadrian. The inside
of the Pantheon in cross-section consists of a
circle inscribed on a square. Its hemispherical
dome, resting on a cylindrical tambour the height
of which is equal to the radius of the dome,
constitutes a clear, geometric figure which is
elegant and balanced. The dome of the Pantheon,
the oldest surviving dome from antiquity, crosses
over a clearing of 42.5 metres with a maximum
thickness of 7 metres at the base and 60
centimetres close to the 'oculus', divided in such
a way that the tensile stresses are below the
concrete resistance. Only a few fissures have
appeared in the chambers during its 18 centuries
of existence, such is the strength provided by the
double roof of poured concrete together with a
system of arches and meridians. The inside of the
dome is lined with panelling of four steps, the
dimensions of which decrease gradually as they
approach the crown.

**Figure 2.26**
Section of Agrippa's
Pantheon.

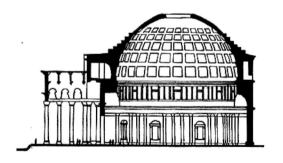

**Figure 2.27**
An example of a
dome with an oculus.
© Alfonso Ramirez

The dome is crowned by the 'oculus', a circular, open aperture through which light may penetrate, creating a mystic atmosphere in the temple. The clearing covered by the dome of the Pantheon was unequalled for more than 1300 years until the octagonal dome of the cathedral in Florence exceeded it by just 90 centimetres at its maximum clearing.

## Byzantium architecture and its majestic basilica

The basic characteristics of Byzantine architecture are found in different roots: in the grandeur of the imperial Roman style, and in the oriental style.

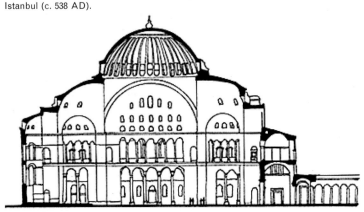

First was the dilemma of how to use the vault to cover large public spaces, and this involved another completely unsolved problem: how to build it supported on a square or rectangular base. This challenge was solved by using the pendentive or squinch. Pendentives, of Persian origin, consist of making the angles of the square eight-sided by using small arches with a conical shape. In squinches, a Byzantine creation, curved and triangular supports fill the space between the angles of the base and the springer of the vault's circle. Squinches are still found today in the cross-vaults of Renaissance and baroque churches.

Another notable feature of Byzantine architecture is the heightening of the Roman arch to become the characteristic Byzantine arch. Marble and mosaics were also used to cover the façades and the interior walls of churches. The floor plan of the Byzantine temple was based on the Greek cross, and had a dome at the end of each of its four arms and over the intersection. Under the rule of Justine in the sixth century, Byzantine architecture reached full maturity in the largest Christian church ever built, St Sophia in Istanbul (Constantinople).

With 40,000 workers divided into teams of 440 men, St Sophia was built with lightning speed in only five years. The problem of the roof of St Sophia was boldly solved by architects Antemio de Tralles and Isidoro de Mileto, who introduced a novel way of using domes. The domes were divided in half and supported by a barrel vault; the resulting vaults became two large apses that produced an ample, elongated space inside. The relation between the height and the diameter of the dome – 16 metres by 31 metres – gives St Sophia its exceptional, unique interior space. Light plays a predominant role. The sense of light within the dome and its ascension upwards are attained by means of an infinite gradation of dark areas, from the shadows at floor level up to the luminous crown. The proportions and harmony found in St Sophia moved Procopio of Cesarea, the historian of the period, to say: **'Whoever enters there to pray immediately comprehends that this work could not have been realised by mere human strength or ability, but by the grace of God.'**[16]

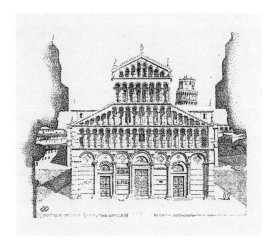

## Romanesque and its field of miracles

The Byzantine period was followed by the Romanesque, which flowered in territories devastated and isolated by the barbarian invasions.

On the feudal horizon of an impoverished, agrarian society, the nerve centres were the churches and convents. Chronicles of the tenth and eleventh centuries are full of stories about fires that burned churches – protected with wooden supports and roofing – down to the ground in just a few hours. To prevent this kind of disaster, wood had to be substituted with stone. The problem of how to build vaults on an entire religious site was the technical and unvarying challenge faced by the Romanesque architect.

One constant in the churches was their floor plan in the shape of a Latin cross, essentially made up of a longitudinal nave, two transepts with arches and round-arched barrel vaults, and a dome placed between them. Their origin was in the fusion of two distributive systems: the Byzantine floor plan and primitive Christian architecture. The lateral naves perform the function of absorbing the stress to the exterior walls and projecting counter-forts created by the arches, and balancing the structure as a whole. The groined arches, inherited from Rome, were formed by two perpendicular barrel vaults that cut across each other diagonally, divided into four parts which set their load on to four pillars. These vaults allowed for windows, making the structure lighter and sunnier. The supports of such vaults rest on transverse arches – known as

**Figure 2.30**
Detail of a rose window typically found in Gothic cathedrals. This one is situated inside Notre-Dame cathedral church, Île de la Cité, Paris, France. Begun in 1163, Notre-Dame is an exceptional example of Gothic architecture and should be particularly noted for its thirteenth-century stained-glass rose windows and flying buttresses. © Leo de Wys.

reinforcing arches or ribs – and on longitudinal arches. The final result was a union of supports and out-thrusts.

Surface decoration accentuated lines and planes, mixing together motifs such as zigzags, eight-petalled flowers and spirals. These were influenced by oriental embroidery, Grecian frets, grapes, pearls, Asiatic heads and dragons, griffins, lions, Persian vegetation and, lastly, Muslim elements such as arches intercrossed with black-and-white stone, elaborate modillions, and even Kufic writing.

An example of developed Romanesque architecture is found in the 'Field of Miracles' in Pisa, Italy. It is a group of buildings including a cathedral, a baptistery, a cemetery, and its famous leaning campanile. The cathedral managed to attain harmony in spite of the many interruptions that occurred during its construction. Its varied architectural influences included the Lombards, Arabs and Armenians as well as Romanesque and classic architecture. Construction took nearly 200 years and the result is a robust, imposing structure that constituted both the beginning and the culmination of architecture in Pisa. This cathedral marks the gentle transition from the Romanesque to the Gothic, illustrated by many Gothic details introduced naturally during the final phase of construction of the cathedral, baptistery and campanile.

## Gothic architecture and its unfinished cathedral

The thirteenth century passed. As a consequence of the expressive possibilities resulting from new structural forms, the Gothic style arose, more refined and bold than the Romanesque.

The defining characteristics of the Gothic style are the pointed arches (ogives), the vault and the sharp steeple, as well as the ability to conquer heights previously unimagined. Multicoloured stained-glass windows give its spacious interiors a peculiar kaleidoscopic illumination.

The crossing of diagonal arches made the construction and the centring of the vault easier, decreasing the cost of expensive scaffolds and making the laying and hardening of the mortar safer. It also reinforced the vault at its weak points, along the groins and in the upper planes. The pointed arch, unlike arches formed by a precise semicircle, made it possible to increase the height because the structure was raised more rapidly and had an application point located at the thrust-stresses of the vaults. The combination of pillars, abutments and flying buttresses kept the building upright by relieving the weight, thus obtaining agile, dynamic shapes and a balance of stresses and forces.

These are imposing structures that convey a sense of balance and rhythm in their multilateral journey skywards. Writings of the period echoed this: since God creates all things, people should strive to return to God through those things by means of height.

Gothic cathedrals are the archetype of Gothic architecture. Their naves reach heights of 20 to 50 metres and have natural light. The marvellous stained-glass windows give life to the whole edifice. These windows predominate over the walls and take the place of mural paintings. They offer the cathedrals forms of expression unknown until then.

These cathedrals do not hide the stresses and tensions necessary to achieve the spatial transfiguration of both the interior and exterior, but convert them into expressive elements topped off by sculptural, ornamental forms. They use sumptuous portals with recessed arches decorated with legions of angels, saints and demons.

The Cathedral of Notre-Dame in Paris is the birthplace and compendium of all Gothic cathedrals. The history of Notre-Dame began in 1163 when the first cornerstone was laid. By 1196, the chorus and the naves were practically completed, suggesting that the cathedral would be finished in just a few more years. Nevertheless, the work went on until 1345, perfecting that already done.

Between 1845–1864 Viollet Le Duc, a genius of restoration, returned Notre Dame to its original splendour, remaking statues, eaves, structures and adornments, and restoring the rose-windows and other glass windows. Even then the cathedral was not finished, as some spires were still missing.

**Figure 2.31**
Elevation of Santa
María de la Fiore,
Florence, Italy
(thirteenth century).

**Figure 2.32**
Structural system of
Brunelleschi's dome
(fifteenth century).

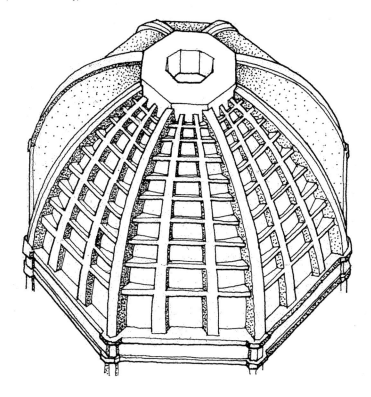

## The renaissance and its Florentine dome

The great heights which Gothic architecture
achieved suited the mysticism of the medieval
period. However, during the fifteenth and
sixteenth centuries, the cultural and artistic
movement of the Renaissance appeared in Italy.
The Renaissance combined several of the
technical and aesthetic achievements of the
Middle Ages, but returned to the horizontal
direction of architecture based on the dome.
Renaissance humanism included such
protagonists as Leonardo da Vinci,
Michaelangelo, Brunelleschi, Alberti and
Bramante, among others.

Renaissance thinkers looked at nature in a
different way. It ceased to be a simple revelation
of God and became part of the universe with
humans at the centre. The study of the human
body became very important and this influenced
decisions in design. It probably contributed to the
reappearance of the church with a centralised
floor plan; it may also have caused the obsession
of Renaissance architects with the circle and
sphere, as both were considered harmonious
elements. Leonardo da Vinci used to say: '**I
always begin with a circular shape because it
is more perfect than any other.**'[17]

Aesthetically, the Renaissance was a re-
evaluation of the simple, rational shapes of
Roman classicism beginning with a rigorous
study of proportions based on geometric ratios.
This study brought about achievements of
admirable harmony in the development of a new
kind of architecture made by humans, for
humans. This made it possible for Renaissance
architecture, unlike Gothic, to move on from the
church to public and residential buildings. The
ideal use of space gradually became less sacred
and more human.

Renaissance architecture really began with
the Florentine dome of Santa María de la Fiore
and ended with the Roman dome of St Peter's
Basilica, Vatican City, Rome. With the execution
of the former, Brunelleschi was architecturally
transforming Florence from a medieval town into
the capital of the Renaissance period. The history
of the erection of this dome is particularly
important in understanding the creative soul that
illuminated that period.

**Figure 2.33**
Interior of Santa
María Tonantzintla,
Puebla, Mexico
(eighteenth century).

In 1294 Arnulfo Di Cambio began work on the cathedral. He was replaced by Francisco Talenti, in 1357, who completed the octagonal tambour that would support the dome. By 1415 notice was circulated asking for bids to build the dome. The greatest architects of the period participated, but no winner was found. The general consensus was that the dome was too large and construction would be hampered by too many conditions. However, in 1418 Brunelleschi made a revolutionary proposal saying that the dome could be constructed without a wooden framework and he suggested presenting a brick model to prove it. This was taken so seriously that they paid him for the model even though they knew that such a large dome had never before been constructed without temporary supports.

Brunelleschi's new approach was made up of many components, the most important of which was its double dome of masonry – a thin, interior octagonal shell connected by vertical ribs to another even thinner one on the outside. Nine horizontal rings made of sandstone reinforced with iron chains prevented the collapse of the dome under the enormous tension of its parallels and its tendency to rupture at the edges. These elements have meant that the dome has remained undamaged for six centuries, unlike other great domes of antiquity such as those of St Sophia and St Peter's, both of which required later repairs. The eight large ribs that begin in the angles of the octagon and the 16 small ribs placed between them constitute the frame of the dome. The ribs maintain their width, but their depth diminishes as they near the upper octagon, which serves as a cornerstone for all 24 ribs and as support for the magnificent *cimborrio* (lantern).

The simplicity of the dome's external appearance belies the revolutionary method of construction: both the 24 ribs and the two domes (internal and external) had to reach the same height simultaneously during construction, adding to the difficulty of completing the upper rings at the same time as the ribs. All of these work structurally only when they are complete. Brunelleschi solved these problems with knowledge and imagination, conceiving these three central rings as perfect circles in such a way that even though the dome is octagonal, it works like a circular dome structurally yet remained stable throughout its construction. The uppermost ring acts like a brace for the vertical arches.

The problem posed by the rings was solved by creating a fishbone design in the masonry, interlacing bricks vertically which followed a spiral curve, with the horizontal ones resting on the finished lower ring. In doing this, Brunelleschi managed to prevent the lower ring from sliding and to secure each new layer under construction to three under-layers that supported the inside pressure of the vertical arches reclining on them. He was thereby able to construct the largest dome ever built without the help of the framework inside. The construction was completed in 1436.

## The Baroque and its Mexican church

Also originating in Italy, the baroque (meaning 'irregular pearl') period followed the Renaissance period. It began with a movement known as mannerism, a style strongly supported by the great masters of the Renaissance. Young artists and architects of the sixteenth century had profoundly mixed emotions. They had two options: the first was to imitate the old classic models – in other words, work in the same fashion as Leonardo da Vinci, Michaelangelo, Brunelleschi, and others; the second, which most decided to follow, consisted of breaking the rules of order and proportion established during the Renaissance. In one sense, mannerism may be considered the end of the Renaissance and the beginning of the baroque.

The baroque period opened the way to a violent world of forms, a bubbly, undulating filling of space. Walls became contorted, bending and exaggerating their relief. Twisted columns and frontispieces were superimposed. Mouldings wrapped around volutes resembled majestic scenes of reverberating light and shadow. Examples abound, from the artistry of plants and old structures by Borromini to the sumptuous, audacious tones of Velázquez's brush. There is no better example of this period, however, than Mexican churches where baroque art, brought to America by the Spaniards but appropriated by the natives, produced a marvel of artistic outburst. The church of Santa María Tonantzintla in the state of Puebla is one of the most representative works of sacred Mexican art, a product of American cultural syncretism. '**Tonantzintla is an Indian recreation of the Indian paradise, white and golden. The chapel is a cornucopia of abundance in which all the fruits and**

**flowers of the tropics ascend toward the dome, toward the dream of infinite abundance**',[18] as Carlos Fuentes aptly described it.

The simple tower and multicoloured façade of this church, covered with bricks, keep one from guessing what marvels are inside. The floor plan of the building is simple and can be seen from the entrance underneath the chorus, as well as from the doors of the baptistery and lateral chapels. Directly in front of the nave, the transepts and the apse are covered by the dome, which is crowned with a lantern and reinforced by four windows that light the central area.

The effect, so simply expressed in words, is totally different when entering the church. An interior of such complexity and blinding, polychromatic effect makes it difficult to find words to describe it. It is like penetrating a vibrant jungle that holds a collection of forms in relief – flowers, faces, heads, saints, cherubs – all edged in gold leaf, covering the vaults, arches, walls and pilasters, enveloping whoever enters the church with its playful charm in a poetic interaction of cultural and historical images.

People began to tire of the ornamental excesses of rococo. At the same time they were exhausted by the feelings of idealism and freedom that the independence of the United States and the French Revolution had encouraged. A reaction occurred and an interest in ancient classicism was reborn. The neo-classical period began, during which a great number of buildings, reminiscent of those built by the Greeks and Romans, were constructed. This lasted until around 1830, when the Gothic and *Romantic* styles were added to the classical styles, along with elements from oriental cultures that had developed separately from the European, such as those from China, Japan, India and other countries.

This was the beginning of a new era called *Romanticism* that expressed itself eclectically in architecture. This style took what it wanted from anywhere as long as it was adjustable to its needs. The *Romantic* period lasted until the middle of the nineteenth century, when iron structures appeared.

The modern city

### Antecedents

For thousands of years people in vernacular society have constructed their own homes and buildings in keeping with their antecedents, environment and needs. This has resulted in harmonious human dwellings and populations that have kept their unity through the years. Even today there are cities that have not been affected by industrial expansion and have maintained their old nucleus and physical structure. Such is the case of Venice, Siena and Carcassonne.

During the twentieth century, however, cities have generally experienced the most radical, rapid transformations in history. Factories, workshops and industries were established in them, not to mention buildings of the new economic order like banks, offices and commercial organisations. The need for manual labour in industry and the lack of economic stimulus in the countryside led to an uninterrupted flow of people to the city. Cities have had to spread out at a rapid rate without any time to control their own development. Consequently, in most of these cities, spaces for people to gather together and the unity characteristic of vernacular settings have been lost. Worse still, the growth has accelerated, becoming more uncontrolled, more miserable and more chaotic.

6 The pyramids were designed for eternity, the cathedrals thought to last centuries, the speculative building of today will, perhaps, be demolished within 20 years 9

Wilirom, *Structure, The Essence of Architecture* [19]

**Figure 2.34**
Comparison of the street plans and housing density between a city of the Middle East and a Western city. (a) Maps of the constructed area, (i) Baghdad 100 m; (ii) suburbs, USA 100 m; (b) maps of the streets, (i) Baghdad 100 m; (ii) suburbs, USA 100 m.

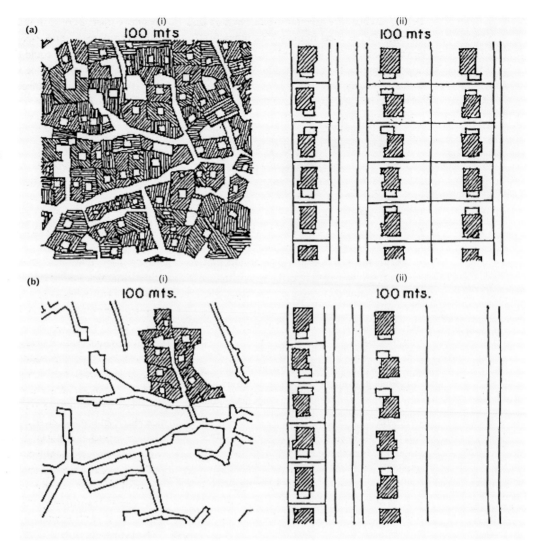

As already mentioned, human settlements are a relatively new phenomenon and were preceded by a long period during which they were nomadic. The first sedentary civilisations were the result of agricultural communities that settled in fertile valleys close to large rivers, hence the name 'potemic' civilisations. To cite the better-known cases, Mesopotamians settled around the delta formed by the Euphrates and Tigris Rivers; Indian civilisation developed in the valleys of the Indus and Ganges Rivers; Egyptian culture flourished along the Nile; the Chinese settled in the zone formed by the deltas of the Hwang-Ho and Yang-tze Rivers.

As time passed, oriental cities commonly followed a labyrinth-like pattern, with narrow streets designed to provide shade. Generally positioned in a north-south direction, these streets had generous but irregular sidewalks

shaded by the canopies of buildings that housed stores and workshops. In contrast, those people who lived in the little alleys positioned in an east-west direction following the sun's path, built eaves on their façades to protect them from the sun. Northerly winds followed the main streets and, at intersections, produced changes in pressure that created a suction of air up the narrow streets. Western visitors thought the entangled streets and lanes were chaotic, although actually there was a hidden logic and the urban order was much more sophisticated than they realised. Even today these towns are characterised by a succession of private, semi-private, semi-public and public spaces governed by a clear hierarchical arrangement.

The concept of a central patio originated in primitive villages where a group of houses would be built around an open, fenced area, as with the

Dogones. Thus, the oriental urban dwelling had its origin in the rural home with a patio. In Egypt, the patio is the central nucleus around which domestic life revolves. This idea passed on to Mesopotamia and later spread throughout the Islamic World, where the so-called eastern house with a patio has remained customary for more than 200 consecutive generations.

In North Africa and the Far East, where climatic conditions are much the same, similar solutions were adopted to obtain comfortable microclimates inside the houses. The concept of the patio with fountains originated here. Besides its aesthetic appeal, the water from the fountain cooled and humidified the air through evaporation. This, together with ornamental plants, provided moist, refreshing air that contrasted with the dust and heat of an arid climate.

The patio is the heart of the house. The Chinese define it as the 'gift from heaven' that provides their homes with air, light and rainwater. Besides the climatic advantages, it gives visual, acoustic and psychological privacy. The patio became a pleasant central point to which all inside rooms had a view. The indoor façades were decorated while those facing the street were simple; there were only a few windows with latticed shutters so that the inhabitants could see out without being seen. The distribution of indoor areas was irregular, modest, simple and flexible, with very little

**Figure 2.35**
Illustration showing the patio of a house in Cairo, Egypt.

furniture apart from rush matting to sit on, pillows to sleep on, and shelves on which to put things. Rich and poor could live happily together because there were no showy exteriors.

Ancient oriental civilisations preceded western civilisations by more than 5000 years. They first influenced the West through Greek and Roman civilisations, which created the classic urban home with a central patio. This spread with Christianity. After the fall of the Roman Empire, only a few Byzantine cities survived wars and plagues. On the Iberian Peninsula, Cordoba, Granada, Toledo, and Palermo in southern Italy, kept their oriental lifestyle until the Arabs were expelled at the end of the fifteenth century. Besides these places and Byzantium (Constantinople) that blossomed during the high Middle Ages, the idea of building around a patio was continued in the convents and monasteries of the Christian church.

Many medieval houses also had a central patio, but its function was different – the central patio area became a service area used for loading and unloading, for craftsmen's workspaces, or it was transformed into orchards. The rooms faced the street and looked over a back patio that usually served as a stable. As time passed, this housing plan became the pattern in the urban western world, except in those areas where Moorish influences continued.

In a time of growing insecurity, defence was the main concern when building houses, rather than the indoor temperature, as had previously been the case. Towers appeared in early medieval houses. Some people abandoned their cities of origin and looked for places that would provide natural protection. They founded cities like Venice, Arles, and Dubrovnik. The typical city of that time was surrounded by defensive walls and a moat with one or two watch towers flanking the entrance gates. Because of topography, the shape of the city resulted in a natural, organic growth that tended to be circular. There was usually a cathedral or a monastery in the centre. According to Norbert Shoenawer, the layout of these cities was formed: '**by narrow, serpentine, picturesque, irregular lanes that became wider here and there, creating small squares. It is hard for a modern citizen who has never seen a medieval city to imagine the quality of those physical spaces in this type of city.**'[20] The wall was the unmistakable barrier that marked the end of the rural area and the beginning of the city – of conquered space, and of security.

**Figure 2.36**
The Roman walled
city of Arles.

The expansion of cities was internal: they grew upwards, not outwards. This contributed to a growth in the number of small cities. During the fourteenth century, gunpowder became very important, to the point where the defensive walls of a city were almost redundant. The Black Plague reared its head in Europe and caused the death of nearly half the total population.

During the sixteenth century factors of military importance and the need to use vehicles with wheels meant that changes were essential. In Renaissance times some cities were constructed and governed by the following principles of planning: straight, wide avenues and streets; an urban layout in the shape of a chess board; and the use of plazas or squares, not only for monuments or as areas for markets, but with a domestic character as well. Although the aristocracy changed their lifestyle, craftspeople and labourers retained some habits from the Middle Ages. The shopkeeper, therefore, lived above the establishment, and the artisan worked from home.

The social strata in England began to experience changes. Since middle-class families could not occupy palaces, they lived in imposing terraced houses with façades disguised as palaces.

At the beginning of the seventeenth century, Henri IV planned the first of the residential squares in France: La Place Royale (now called Place des Voges). The goal of the project was to move the homes of the aristocracy closer to that of the king and recreate the pomp of the court in the middle of Paris. This square was also conceived as a centre for cosmopolitan life within the congested city. The square, with 38 three-storey buildings, was used in the beginning for tournaments and contests. Afterwards it became a plaza with a statue of Louis XIII in the middle, and still later it was transformed into a fenced park, surrounded by narrow streets for access. The concept of a residential square was a novel idea quickly adopted by other aristocracy.

This semi-public park in the square functioned like a large garden. There, in full view of the public, the family carried out their recreational activities, while the rear service patios were maintained in their houses. This style influenced the United States where the first cities founded incorporated the concept of the square and the reticular outline. The first city to apply these concepts to urban life was Philadelphia. Planned in 1683 by Thomas Hulme, the city comprised, besides the main square, four more squares of lesser size for the recreation of future citizens. In 1733 James Oglthorpe and his 116 colonists adapted the concept of residential squares for their new cities.

This new lifestyle produced an unprecedented change: the urban home was separated from the workplace, and women lost continuous contact with their husbands. The family, as a basic social unit, suffered a tremendous setback. To quote Mumford: '**The city became a no-man's land**.'[21]

The separation of productive work and domestic activities contributed new characteristics to buildings and neighbourhoods: the city was divided into commercial, residential, industrial, and recreational zones. In this way, the Industrial Revolution was a decisive factor in affecting western urban housing. Initially, given that the function of machines depended on the energy produced by the movement of water, most industries were located close to rivers. These first industrial buildings were constructed using wood and stone and, next to the residential housing, they constituted urban entities with roots in natural resources. The river became the energy source for industry and the main street was for commerce and transportation, and also served as a recreational space.

The Industrial Revolution entered its second phase when coal replaced water as a source of energy. Industries began moving to wherever the mineral was abundant. This expansion brought with it a special kind of migration. Labourers from the country moved into areas close to industry because no fast, cheap transportation was available. The new worker did not grow food and had to learn to depend solely on his salary. Housing was located in the middle of the grimy industrial environment of factories. Inhabitants stopped sharing heterogeneous, socio-cultural stories and experiences; the rich and poor no longer went to the same churches or schools or shops.

The exploitation of urban land at the end of the nineteenth century culminated in its division into small crowded lots. A great many builders embarked on speculative adventures, building terraced houses tightly together with façades facing the street and tiny patios at the back. In some cases groups of ten or twenty houses were built, in rows one next to the other, all with identical floor plans and façades.

The size of the houses was gradually reduced. Some wealthy families abandoned their houses in the deteriorating cities in England and gave rise to a new kind of dwelling: 'the manor.' Those in other countries, principally the United States where there was plenty of land, did the same. The American pioneer, Andrew Jackson Downing, a prestigious landscape architect in Europe, built a house on the banks of the Hudson River for his wife and himself. It was positioned in such a way that you couldn't see the village from the house, and the valley panorama gave the impression of being part of his property. Downing visited New York constantly due to his work and some city dwellers decided to emulate his move to a more tranquil, healthy and agreeable environment. The attachment with the city was not broken, however, since these manors continued to depend on commercial activities. Suburbs proliferated around the city. The outside façades reflected the social level of the occupants, resulting in pretentious homes that, from size and building materials, could be interpreted as symbols of success.

From the end of the nineteenth century, technological development was favoured. This, together with progress in communication, produced the Bauhaus, the incubation of a movement called the 'modern' or 'international' style that has experienced unmatched development. Modern architecture is characterised by the kind of buildings that began to be constructed around 1910 and evolved in the period between the First and Second World Wars. The layouts of cities then showed rationality and order; the iron and reinforced concrete were free of ornamentation. Little interest was shown in the physical and mental well being of occupants, and a separation was made between historic styles.

**Figure 2.37**
(a) and (b) Views of
typical modern cities.

(a)

(b)

After the Second World War this movement in architecture spread throughout the world. The more the process of industrialisation advanced, the better the urban environment became in some aspects and the worse it became in others. Cities grew, the standard of living rose, but new problems appeared as well. From 1960, this movement in architecture exaggerated the international style and emphasised the image of technology in buildings. Many people found them monotonous and cold. Charles Jencks in his book *The Language of Post-Modern Architecture* comments: '**Modern architecture was extinguished with one blow and one loud explosion..., it died in St. Louis, Missouri, July 15, 1972, at 3:32 in the afternoon when** several blocks of the infamous Pruitt-Igoe Project were given the *coup de grâce* by dynamite, a final blow. It had previously been the object of vandalism, mutilation, and defecation on the part of its inhabitants..., although millions of dollars were reinvested in an attempt to keep them alive..., an end was finally made to their misery. Boom, boom, boom.'[22]

## The contemporary city

Architecture has to be relevant to its historical time; it cannot be otherwise. Therefore, according to Ronald Conrad, structures created by humans: 'evolved toward abstraction and the geometric influenced by theories of numbers and line.'[23] The development of mathematics, especially of Newtonian physics, played a determining role in modern cities. The ruler, the square and the right angle displaced all other shapes. Geometric form rose up to 'rationalise' spaces. Analytical geometry left the abstract world of theory and began to take the form of homes, factory workshops, public buildings and so on. Cities were drawn with a ruler. 'Nature stopped being the great teacher of humanity',[24] Conrad Ronald tells us with certainty. Now science has taken its place: 'only what is founded on purely quantitative relationships is valid. Whatever cannot be measured or explained does not exist.'[25]

Cities are cut from the same pattern. The basic principles of modern urban architecture are practically the same in Bonn and Buenos Aires, Montreal and Madrid, Mexico City and Rome, St Petersburg and even cities in Africa. Buildings are constructed with parallelepipedons, streets and avenues plough furrows through, and divide, squares. Hospitals, prisons, houses, large shopping centres, public buildings, and apartment blocks are all boxed up. Size has become a premise and similarity a virtue.

Not only does modernity identify us, it has homogenised us. Cities have determined our way of life; our lives have not shaped the cities. Teenagers, whether in London or in the United States, dress almost alike, seek the same diversions, and pursue very similar ideals. 'Whoever is not like everyone else, who does not think like everyone else, runs the risk of being eliminated',[26] wrote Ortega y Gasset, referring to the modern masses. And perhaps we should add that all architecture that is not measured by the axiom of the square runs the same risk.

## Architecture as merchandise

Capitalism, business and accounting touch all of our activities. The historic role of capitalists was totally revolutionary: they shook society out of the lethargy of the Middle Ages; centralised the means of production; submitted to the State; subordinated the peasants; and created cities.

The basis of capitalism is merchandise – goods that are produced to be sold. The production of merchandise has its own rules: a rational technique, assembly line production, job specialisation, hierarchical organisation, income-yield capacity, and so forth. These rules were imposed on society, in interpersonal relationships. The city was planned and developed under capitalist dogma; the tool was called 'merchandise architecture.'

Housing is a clear example of how the canons of assembly line production have dominated architecture and urbanism. If at the beginning there was a tendency to unify styles, now we see block after block covered with identical buildings. Starting with the Industrial Revolution, modular planning has intensified.

In *The Seven Lamps of Architecture* (1855), John Ruskin declared that: 'the architect who is not a sculptor or painter is no more than a frame-maker on a large scale.'[27] Frank Lloyd Wright wrote in his *Testament* that modern cities were sample collections of 'automobile radiators', 'bird cages' and 'zoological showcases'.[28]

The city of Detroit once paid Frank Lloyd Wright a large sum of money to diagnose its problems and suggest a programme of urban renewal. After several months of study and research, Wright told the authorities at a special board meeting: 'I suggest you tear down everything and begin again. Perhaps this ought to be the way to rejuvenate the suburbs, as well as the ghettos of the city'.[29]

Another trait of capitalism is super-specialisation – the extreme division of labour – and this has been developing in architecture too. The integral builder of the past who both planned and constructed is an anachronism. There is now what Felix Candela says is: 'the absurd dismemberment of work in architecture, engineering, and contracting'.[30] It is absurd, too, because what was done at the beginning to

**Figure 2.38**
Model of a modern city made with rubbish.

improve the quality of the work has ended up being a disadvantage: integral design remains outside the domain of all three branches.

Since the First World War, architects have complicated building plans and specified everything down to the last detail as never before. Until 1900, it was the norm for them to draw a quick sketch or diagram, presenting a model for only the most complicated buildings. Builders took the design and built it to the best of their ability.

In recent years building contractors have no part in the creative process, merely carrying out commands. They follow precise instructions from pages of drawings, with no chance to place even one nail where they think it convenient.

The African peasant could never imagine the ritual necessary to build an urban house. Estate agents, lawyers and local authorities are involved in buying the land. Drawings need to be

prepared, estimates made, and other bureaucratic procedures gone through to get licences and obtain loans or mortgages before building can start. Even when the house is finished taxes, insurance and other fees have to be paid.

Profit is now the goal: everything that generates profit is seen as good. The beauty of a building is not as important as its income-yield capacity. Once good value became the essence, buildings with no aesthetic appeal whatsoever began to go up.

Simultaneously, the spirit of greed threw out any kind of ecological consideration: water, earth, and air contamination are everywhere. It is probable that at this very moment you see, hear, smell, touch, and are swallowing pollution.

Modern cities have been divided in such a way that proletarian marginalised residential areas have been pushed to one side, the upper class bourgeois to another, and the middle class has filled up the rest: '**The city is built in such a way that one can live in it for years and years and ride from one side to the other without finding a marginalised neighbourhood or having contact with them**'[31] noted Engels at the end of the last century.

## A place made of boxes

The design of a modern city is often dependent on three agents that are involved with housing development. The first is the government agency that authorises its construction as long as it 'complies' with a series of regulations. Another is the promoter whose main interest is profit. The last is the city-planning expert who takes into account all the rules, uses and car access, but does not think very much about the human occupant.

The present city is made up of sections divided into large square blocks that are themselves divided into blocks. The work of the architect begins with the space allocated, which being rectangular generally makes the house boxy. The box-like house is made up of rectangular prisms each meant for a specific function.

*Boxes and a square grid... these are the basic ingredients of a western city in our times, and now we cannot make a city without them. All we need are a piece of chalk and a bin full of rubbish; in five minutes we can construct a model. The recipe is simple: take the chalk and draw a large grid subdivided into squares. Then empty the bin. You can use a shoe box for a hospital or, if you like, a prison; a few milk cartons and you have an apartment block; that biscuit box will be perfect for a theatre; glue several cigarette boxes together and make a skyscraper; there is a medicine box and you have another block of flats; here you have a Kleenex box and hey presto! an instant public building. With a cereal box you can make a factory, school, or department store.*

At last our model is finished, and we ask what city in the world it might look like. The answer, of course, is obvious! It could look like any city at all. The indiscriminate use of the right angle has limited contemporary architectural imagination. The worst of the problem is that day by day things not only continue unchanged, but they regenerate, they reproduce. As Luna Arroyo says: '**any graduate from any architectural school or institute anywhere... designs every kind of building following well known recipes which are nothing more than the application of the parallelepipedon and the parallelogram as the foundation for every architectural shape.**'[32] The rubbish bin recipe has become a whole school.

We shall try to face the modern urban phenomenon as if we had a panoramic view and were, at the same time, in the city. Let us attempt a general description of the 'place made of boxes', its most puzzling problems, the challenges involved in solving them, and possible solutions.

Viewed from an aeroplane, the earth's surface resembles a patchwork of right-angled shapes and colours. Everything works as a grid: fields are ploughed in parallel lines; towns and cities are criss-crossed with roads irrespective of the natural contours of the land. On descent, the grid becomes three-dimensional, buildings meet and rise, one after another. As Friedensreich Hundertwasser would say, the city is '**a jungle made of straight lines**'.[33]

Most modern cities have become places for things, not for people, and currently buildings themselves prevent good ventilation. There is air pollution caused by factories and fuel-consuming vehicles, along with human and animal waste. '**What is my child going to breathe when he is born?**' asks Angeles Palomar, a character in *Cristóbal Nonato (Christopher Unborn)*, a novel by Carlos Fuentes. She asks this question because her child is going to be born in Mexico City in 1992. The answer is terrible: '**Mashed crap. Carbonic gas. Metallic dust. And all that at 2300-metres altitude flattened beneath a layer of icy air and surrounded by a prison of encircling mountains: the garbage that imprisons....**'[34]

## Time in a modern city

When the first studies of urban sociology appeared, city planning experts and intellectuals rushed to affirm the undeniable existence of a real city culture. In a very general sense, it could be said that culture is the way in which a certain time and space relate to each other; the conjoining of a population's forms and behaviours. The comprehension of a culture then, depends greatly on the definition one has of the

**Figure 2.39**
Original topography
and network of San
Francisco.

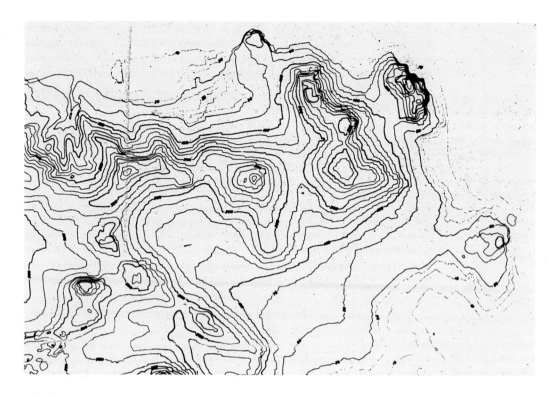

The network advances without respect for the unplanned shapes of the hills.

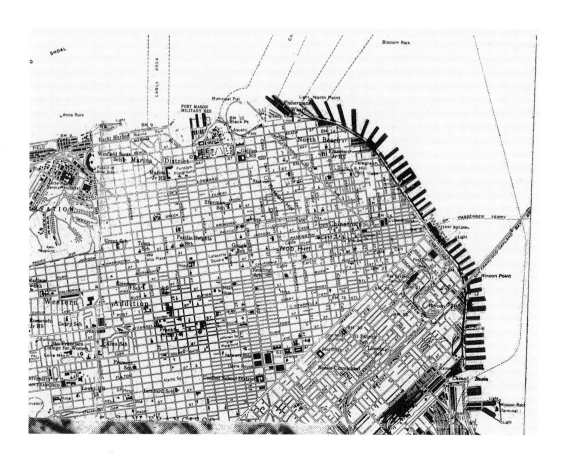

space and the time in which one is growing and developing.

'**...We all felt that time is different: we were in the city where by definition everything goes faster, especially time. Time flies, it gets away from us, but at the same time it weighs heavily on us and drags its feet...**',[35] points out Carlos Fuentes in the novel already mentioned.

Before Christ was born, people perceived time as cyclical. Seasons changed throughout the year. Night and day were two phases of the same circle that appeared not to do anything except spin on its unchanging centre. However, from the moment of Jesus' birth, the West entered fully into historical time. A line of demarcation was drawn before and after and cyclical time disappeared from the human mind. Modernity went even further: '**The Modern Age is the first to exalt change and make it its foundation. Difference, separation, heterogeneity, plurality, evolution, development, revolution, history: all these words can be condensed into one: Future. It is not past times nor eternity, it is not the time that is but rather the time that yet does not exist and is always on the point of being**',[36] explains the Mexican writer Octavio Paz in *The Children of Mud (Los Hijos del Limo).*

Modern humans, especially the urban ones, have made future life their goal, something that is by definition unattainable. The life of people in the city becomes one of constant negation. What the person of the past found in repetitions of yesterday, now always brings with it a denial of what happened yesterday and a race towards the future.

With electricity, the differences between day and night dissolve with the flick of a switch. Active time can continue after dark, and so sensory stimulation for the city dweller never stops. Time in modern cities is always accelerating.

With the evolution of capitalism time itself has needed to be rationalised. It has been restructured, and divided, with periods allocated to different activities. When traffic lights are red, cars must stop; when they're green cars can go. At seven in the morning, we talk about the 'rush hour.' On Sunday night all the roads leading into the city are full. '**In this way the technique of metropolitan life is simply unimaginable without an extremely punctual integration of every activity and mutual relationship to the content of an unvarying, impersonal schedule**',[37] says George Simmel, an urban sociologist. One arrives at the paradox of a time that is both cyclical and historical: urban routine

**Figure 2.40**
Urban Routine.

– a routine that locks us into schedules and chronologies that are both perfectly defined and have perfectly defined boundaries.

## Humans trapped in a box

**The modern city is composed of boxes, and human beings live in these boxes.**

A box is an object that in real life limits us: it locks us up and takes away our freedom. Frank Lloyd Wright describes this in a firmly sarcastic manner: '**Every house is a mechanical forgery of the human body... the whole inside is a sort of stomach that attempts to digest objects,** *objets d'art,* **perhaps, but objects nevertheless. Here is where the feigned affliction installs itself, always hungry for more objects or plethoric because of excess. It seems like the whole life of the common house is a form of indigestion, an unhealthy body that suffers slight illnesses, that demands constant repairs and remedies to survive. It is a marvel that we, its occupants, are not driven crazy in it and with it; perhaps it is a sort of insanity we have put into it.**'[38]

*Here is the story of a man who, like many of us, lived in a modern city: He was born in a room on the fourth floor of a hospital. Born two months premature, he was laid in a little glass box called an incubator. Once at home, he was caged in a crib with brass bars in his bedroom. Time passed, and the little child was installed in a playpen 'to play' – it was square. The child grew, began to crawl, and had his first adventure: he escaped from the playpen, went through the doorway, and arrived at the kitchen where he saw, with wide eyes, a series of integrated boxes. He touched them, left, and entered another box – the dining room. Suddenly through the doorway, he came across a room full of little squares called tiles. He went in and the toilet attracted his attention, perhaps because it was a different shape. After playing with the water for a little while, he returned to a room full of squares and rectangles: electricity sockets, light switches, mirrors, and a series of boxes – furniture, beds, the television set, and so forth. After many attempts, he at last managed to open a drawer and found a box that also contained boxes with smaller boxes inside.*

*Our protagonist grew and attended school. There he was boxed in a classroom. He was given a desk – the third one in the fifth row. Sometimes, to relax, he stopped looking at the blackboard and looked out at the cement patio through a rectangular window. Then he sighed, felt nostalgic, but could not understand why or for what.*

*The man was tenacious and finished a brilliant university career in accounting. He worked in a public office seated in front of a desk and sighed from time to time when, through a window, he observed the city reflected in the mirrored grid of windows on the building opposite... In winter those large, glassed surfaces offered very little protection from the cold; in summer the heat and noise of the streets were oppressive and harried him inside his little cubicle.*

*The man trapped in a box made money, slept in a large, comfortable bed, travelled by car, and bought the largest box in a residential area. This man, from the time he was born, went from one box to another throughout his whole life until he died one afternoon due to acid rain... The last time he was seen, he was in a coffin, the funeral box he was buried in.*

Our home is essential for our formation. Architecture reflects the historical circumstances in which it was produced. The environment acts on us to the same degree that we act on our environment. In our urban surroundings the inhabitant adapts to the house when the opposite should really be the case. Living in order to make (pay for) one's home is not the same as building one's home in order to live in it, as was the case for humans over thousands of years, and which is what the mollusc does. Our homes should allow us to live tranquilly as Barragán dreamed; they should be places where we can read, rest, listen to music, work, paint, meditate, or just be, and not simply suffer, eat, watch television and sleep, as we are accustomed to do.

# THE ORGANIC:
# OUR NATURAL
# SPACE

## 03

❝Style grows like a plant, but it is not the salt that is taken from a sack and sprinkled over those works which in themselves lack flavour❞

Viollet Le Duc[1]

# Organic architecture

During the nineteenth century, architecture lost the sense of direction it had always taken through history. While technology was developing, architecture merely imitated former styles. It was then that art nouveau, a decorative movement prominent from the 1890s to the early 1900s, appeared in Europe. Wanting to be free of anachronistic styles, this movement adopted various manifestations of the twentieth century. Art nouveau had enough energy to get away from the chaotic confusion of historical styles; although influenced by them, it took its own path. Art nouveau and baroque both shared a passion for the biodynamic – the abundance of curves, curled waves and organic motifs in ornamentation, abstract and figurative at the same time.

There was a decided attempt with art nouveau to adopt new materials and techniques, building an original style of architecture.

Concrete, iron and glass, so full of creative possibilities, constituted the pliable mass needed by architects to make the new shapes derived from functions characteristic of these materials. Gabriela Sterner explains: '**All the visual arts found themselves in a harmonious atmosphere which enabled them to prolong their aesthetic pleasure beyond the museum…, managing to compile laws of modern urbanism for the first time: the artist has to create the city, the neighbourhood, the house, the household objects, and the furniture that man uses. Everything should respond to a harmony that enables it to have a re-encounter with the cosmos'.**[2] Moulded ornamentation, repeated many times in façades and furniture, was a particular characteristic. The object should not only express its function through its shape, it should also suggest a mood to the observer: According to Sterner: '**…a chair will be**

**Figure 3.1**
Sketch of a Paris
Métro station
entrance. Hector
Guimard, 1900.

represented as a sprouting plant, as if it were made with stems and flower buds.'[3]

Endell, in his treatise on beauty, explained his process of intuitive creation in the following terms: 'It's like being in a state of drunkenness or insanity that pervades us. Joy threatens to annihilate us; the excessive abundance of beauty asphyxiates us. Whoever has not experienced this will never understand plastic arts. Whoever has never felt ecstatic over random twists of grass, the wonderful loveliness of the leaf of a thistle, the rough youth of buds just opening, who has never felt captivated by and moved to the bottom of his soul by the vigorous line of the roots of a tree, the dauntless strength of cracked bark, the slender softness of a birch, or the infinite quietness in deep foliage, knows nothing at all about the beauty of shape.'[4]

Art nouveau itself became nothing more than a passing gesture but it helped bring about the transition towards the movement of rationalism. Rationalism was based on the simple and functional, but it quickly fell into standardisation and dehumanisation, and into the theoretical and unnatural, creating boxy architecture. Then, as an alternative, so-called organic architecture appeared like an oasis in the desert, more concerned about humans and their environment, more interested in natural, rational and aesthetic shapes. The organic movement includes some of the most celebrated architects of the twentieth century, people who, because of the importance of their work, deserve to be reviewed in more detail, especially since they stand out in a time when their contributions meant swimming against the current.

## Antoni Gaudí: Magic Naturalism

Antoni Gaudí Cornet (1852–1926) was a romantic artist who should be carefully studied with open-mindedness. Originating from the Catalonian region of Spain, he was a man with a Mediterranean spirit, impetuous and sensual. In contrast, he was also a learned European, born under the star of modernity and the critical spirit of rationalism.

Brought up in an atmosphere of Catalonian romanticism, Gaudí developed an open attachment and admiration for everything that looked medieval: castles, monasteries, stone and candles. His ability to analyse and criticise, and especially his profound imagination, made him question the principles of the international school.

Antoni Gaudí's architectural career rose out of a harmonious relationship between the concept of medieval architecture (scholastic) and a modernistic spirit. He took nature – 'the work of the Supreme Architect', as he called it – as his model and archetype. Although inspired by nature, he was not an imitator; if he were a writer, his work would be in line with magical realism.

Some people emphasise the fact that Gaudí, like Joan Miró, found his ideal place of inspiration along the coast near Tarragona, amongst olive and carob trees. It is clear that much of Gaudí's work is saturated by the landscapes there: the colour of the land, the rock formations, the intense light, and the reflections and movements of the sea. Nonetheless they also present us with evidence that, as he himself stated: 'they are sketches..., not literal copies, and they offer distinctively personal drawings inspired by natural shapes....'[6]

> ❝To you who are acquainted with the human skeleton I will say that I study and learn from it because it is made up of structures without any absolute planes, but rather living, bleached shapes ❞
>
> Antoni Gaudí[5]

(a)

(b)

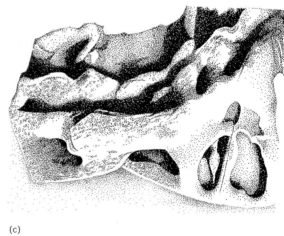

(c)

**Figure 3.2**

(a) Milá House, Barcelona, Spain. Antoni Gaudí, 1906–1910; (b) Milá
House (detail); (c) the rocky formations north of Barcelona influenced
Gaudí's design of the Milá House.

Gaudí's approach was not the passive contemplation of the pure *Romantics* who experienced ecstasy when facing nature, it was more like contemplation accompanied by reflection and imagination: the reflection of the scientist and the imagination of the artist.

Gaudí was impressed by the thoughts and writings of personalities such as Viollet Le Duc and Ruskin. His own work, however, demonstrated a vision and an understanding of authentic plastic-sculptural values that could only have been influenced by sight, not by written arguments. A great part of his work was inspired by everyday objects, often modest things that no one else would really notice. He saw, recorded and transformed these objects into monuments whose origins nobody was able to recognise in his own time because nobody went, as he did, to the source.

Everything in Gaudian plastic art has a place, a function and, like the human body, there is a harmony that blends its different parts so that although they are varied, they all participate in the unity of the finished piece.

Gaudí's greatest quality lies in having an accurate perception of whether a thing should be higher or lower, flatter or more curved. This ability helped him discover that interesting shapes are never flat, but rather concave and convex, a discovery that he made by degrees.

When a real architect is seeking structure, he does not merely look, he observes. Gaudí went beyond contemplation and reached free creation, necessarily passing through a stage where he studied natural shapes – their rhythms, vectorial clash and intrinsic relationships – in minute detail. He believed that architecture was an organic creation, not the arbitrary result of autonomous parts put together. Structure was the central point of his work. Shape, space and function should be appropriate. Gaudí took the skeletons of animals and the dynamics of molluscs and plants, and used them as a guide. He asked himself what gave a feline subtle movements, what made it possible for most clams to combine fragility and submission and what lent a tree its firm, quiet strength. The conclusions he finally drew were truly impressive, and even today bio-engineers are surprised that he was so far ahead of his time. We find examples of this in many of his shapes, which suggest the light concrete shells that we know today.

Another ingredient in his work, counter to intuitive rationality, was sculpture: the magic of shapes. During his last period, Gaudí completely dominated aesthetic shape in the artistic part of his work. In fact, we can go so far as to say that he died when he was just about to make some great discoveries, precisely at the moment when he was starting to incorporate concrete as a new element in his architectural language.

Bringing together structure and sculpture, Gaudí came to believe that buildings should seem cellular and animated. As live beings grow he wanted to design buildings that appeared to grow. To do this he invented an implosive construction for his interiors – advancing curves that broke up and moved rhythmically.

Gaudí took a big step when he slanted the supports, thereby avoiding buttresses that he said were 'Gothic crutches.' He always worked in harmony with the laws of nature and was primordially interested in the internal stresses of the building.

The most representative works by Gaudí can be found in Barcelona. Here we will be referring to a few buildings that accurately represent his style because of their characteristics and tradition in the history of modern architecture.

The Casa Milà, constructed between 1906 and 1910, clearly shows that Gaudí rejected the right angle. In the rough draft, in fact, it is impossible to find straight lines. Perhaps the Casa Milà typifies his free, playful spirit. During its construction and the first years of its existence, it

**Figure 3.2**
(d) Chimneys of the Casa Milà © Alison Yates.

was the object of vigorous controversy that went so far as to insult Gaudí himself. '**But the Casa Milà went ahead, raising its fanciful physiognomy converted into a stone composition, like a concert of organic shapes.**'[7] Inside it is as though the structure is a living organism: undulating and rhythmical, not unlike the Mediterranean waves. The roof with its bizarre chimneys and air ducts resembles an abstract, almost surreal, work of art.

Popularly known as *la pedrera* – 'the quarry' – the Casa Milà is like sand dunes or the silhouette of the hills around Barcelona. In order to achieve that, Gaudí '**clearly gets rid of incorrect, purist constructivism: the whole façade is madness, the structure based on hidden iron ties to hold up the mass of stone molded into shapes as if it were clay....**'[8]

Güell Park can be understood as the dialectic interrelationship between shape and colour, curves and mosaics. The benches have been moulded to the human body. In order to do this, Gaudí sat a nude worker on some plaster grout to make a mould. It is surprising that the movement expressed in this bench could be obtained from prefabricated pieces, starting with vaults made of partitions covered with bits and pieces of ceramic, glass and bottles – extraordinary collages that remind one of abstract and surrealist paintings.

The curvaceous design of Güell Park makes it easier for those watching children play on the terrace to converse. Gaudí's designs are not as abstract and inhuman as they may sometimes appear to be. The needs of people and how they should be met are carefully considered. Perhaps due to his understanding of these needs, Gaudí's work has been accepted by the general public while frequently the most sophisticated sector considers it eccentric.

The Casa Batlló (1904–1906) was, according to Udo Kultermann: '**an architectural work of skin and bones that could have belonged to the world of nomads. Nevertheless all these possibilities for comparison are of a secondary nature; what is more interesting still is the concept of an architectural whole. Like the whole of Gothic art, Gaudí's building forms a unity from a sculptural, pictorial, and architectural point of view.**'[9]

It is impossible to feel indifference towards Gaudí's creations; they are stamped with an imposing spirit that obliges one to stop and contemplate.

(a)

(b)

**Figure 3.3**
(a and b) Güell Park, Barcelona, Spain. Antoni Gaudí, (1900–1914). © Alison Yates.

(a)

**Figure 3.4**
Casa Batlló,
Barcelona, Spain
1904–1906. (a) A detail
of the roof is
reminiscent of the
scales and undulating
movement of snakes;
(b) façade. © Leo de
Wys.

(b)

Casa Vicens (1883–1888) on the Calle de Carlines in Barcelona has contrasting coloured mosaics over stone and brick creating a blend of materials that fills every nook and cranny. Windows with forged iron that looks like twisted vermicelli, and half-moon-shaped balconies that look out over the street, make the whole house appear to be silently yawning. A fusion of Spanish and Arabic styles, the architecture of this building is nothing but unique. The interior is a combination of wood finishes and tiles, the walls decorated with paintings of plants and bird motifs. Ornamentation drips from every ceiling with lavish engravings and stalactite-like forms.

It is said that Picasso took his concept of cubist painting from one of the fireplaces at the Güell Palace. The towers are coloured in a kaleidoscopic fashion: marble, crystal, flowers, and gems are all used in a mosaic – remnants that might have been discarded but have been turned into art. These polychromatic mosaics seem to move with the reflection of the sun.

Situated in a narrow street, it is virtually impossible to get a full view of the palace. Two lavish iron lattice gates welcome the visitor. Inside there is a medieval flavour, but it is medieval with a twist. Gaudí employs parabolic arches that partially obscure the rectangular windows, giving the illusion of arched windows while also restricting the amount of daylight entering the building. The ceilings are ornate with wooden carvings and ironwork. After being under the high roof of the Güell Palace, one goes out into the streets of Barcelona with the feeling of having suddenly awakened from a deep, vivid dream; it is truly a fairy-tale palace.

Gaudí built fancifully at will, but he never played absurd games: his imagination simply played. That is why he was able to let the iron run free and the bars form shapes which beautify the ground with their shadows in the afternoons. How did he accomplish it? We could suggest innate genius, or the artist's optimistic and productive stubbornness, or the faith of a religious person. Certainly each of these played a part.

Antoni Gaudí – genius, artist, mystic – was able to engrave a message into each one of his works, a mood, a project, an ideal. Evidently this implies taking a risk: to be an artist is to bare oneself, to proclaim one's own truth at the top of one's voice with foolish persistence. Following this train of thought, the most 'Gaudian' work is probably the temple of the unfinished Sagrada Familia. Maybe it would be most fitting to forget the rational and analytical explanations for a time and attempt to perceive, to read between the lines, to live the artistic work of Antoni Gaudí.

**Figure 3.5**
The Sagrada Familia (an atonement temple). Antoni Gaudí, 1883–1926. (a) Elevation; (b) interior. © Alison Yates.

(a)

(b)

### Frank Lloyd Wright: Animator of Space

Art history is made up of a succession of cycles. Dissatisfaction with a particular approach surges up and individuals begin to question it and end up making suggestions and proposals. Frank Lloyd Wright did just that: he questioned, proposed, and was innovative.

**Figure 3.6**
(a) Wright was inspired by the pagoda as a vertical element in a group of buildings and used it to integrate the group of laboratory buildings for Johnson Wax. (b) Johnson Wax Building © Architectural Association/Danielle Tinero.

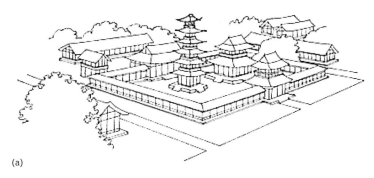

(a)

(b)

His dispute with rationalistic architecture was conclusive: now that 'housing' was being built with quadratic shape, buildings and churches equally parallelepiped, why not once and for all: '**prune the trees, give them a boxy shape, cut them like cubes or triangles, and consequently convert all species into ideal partners for such houses**', comments Frank Lloyd Wright in his book *El Futuro de la Arquitecta*.[11] In the same way he also criticised the divorce between a construction and the land it is built on, between the dwelling and the family that inhabits it.

Wright's proposal was Organic Architecture. 'Organic' must be understood as the unique, the inseparable, the integral. From his first designs, up to the Guggenheim Museum of Art in New York (1956–1959), Wright, an American architect, moved forward to the prototype of organic, integral architecture.

Falling into the temptation of synoptic analysis, we could say that Wright's proposal is based mainly on four fundamental elements: inspiration by nature; oriental influences; reminiscences of the constructions of primitive cultures; and the incorporation of living nature into his work, principally in gardens, patios, and terraces. That is how, inspired by the structural principles of the mushroom, he designed the pillars in the administrative offices of Johnson Wax. The oriental pagoda, on the other hand, inspired the building of the laboratories that served as a plastic contrast to the whole unit.

❛Organic simplicity is the only kind of simplicity that can answer that strange, compelling question for us: Now what, architecture?❜

Frank Lloyd Wright[10]

**Figure 3.7**
Frank Lloyd Wright used the structural principles of the mushroom for the design of the interior pillars in the administrative offices of Johnson Wax, Racine, Wisconsin, USA, 1936–1939. (a) Mushroom © Alejandro Martinez Mena; (b) Johnson Wax Interior © Architectural Association/James Sinclair.

Later, Wright recovered the principles of vernacular architecture found in primitive cultures. Thus, '...The contours of his houses are rounded out with curves,' explains Giedion, 'conforming to the environment and devoid of right angles, similar to the oval Minoan Cretan houses built around 1500 BC or the Mesopotamian farmhouses of 4000 to 2000 BC.'[12]

Such is the case of the 1948 dwelling named The Solar Hemicycle, which uses this solution to protect the house from the strong winds and bitter cold of Wisconsin. Wright was guided by the same instinct that moves you when you feel the force of a strong wind: you turn your back to it and hunch over. He turned the back of the house to the north using a semicircular talus (slope) of earth, which is an excellent thermal mass that deflects the wind, considerably decreasing the energy expenses. The front outlook of the house, with a semicircular shape, is through large bay windows over an enclosed garden. This garden gets plenty of sunshine in winter and provides shade in summer. The Jacobses, the owners of the house, remember that when Frank Lloyd Wright showed them the design, he told them that even if the strongest winds slammed against the back of the house, they would be able to spend the afternoon on the front terrace quietly, enjoying the garden; Mr Jacobs would be able to light his pipe without the slightest problem. And that is exactly what they did...

The Solar Hemicycle can be considered an ecological home with applied ecosystems. The integration of nature and the ornamentation and structure of the house itself make it a model for any building inspired by the principles of organic architecture.

(a)

(b)

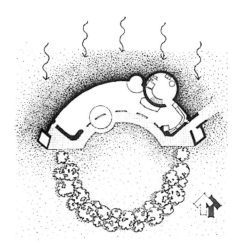

**Figure 3.8**
The Solar Hemicycle, H. Jacobs' House, Frank Lloyd Wright, 1943.

## Juan O'Gorman: Architecture of the Roots

One important exponent of contemporary organic architecture is Juan O'Gorman of Mexico. As a member of the generation of artists that emerged after the 1910 civil war in Mexico, together with Diego Rivera, Orozco, and Siqueiros, O'Gorman always demonstrated a preference for art that was based on experience, concerned about its environment, and dynamic by nature, but to get there, he had to go through several stages of development.

After designing buildings based on the more rigid principles of functionalism, from 1949 O'Gorman began to base his drawings on fundamentals of the organic school, using specifically Frank Lloyd Wright and Antoni Gaudí as his examples.

Of all the advocates of the organic school, he put special emphasis on the desire to link his artistic work with the cultural tradition of its birthplace and its geography. O'Gorman defines organic architecture as: '**an artistic manifestation that is directly related to the geography and history of its place of construction.**'[13]

'Architecture,' then, '**becomes the harmonious instrument between man and the environment where the architectural work is executed..., between the building and its surroundings. According to this architectural concept, human housing becomes the means of providing harmony between man and the earth. Furthermore, we must admit, whether we like it or not, that throughout all of history (especially during the great periods of plastic art) from the most ancient cultures of the Mediterranean to the most archaic of the Americas or the age of the rise of a capitalist society, architecture always walked hand in hand with painting and sculpture, sometimes completely integrated and other times simply decorating it.**'[14]

In 1938 O'Gorman left architecture to dedicate himself totally to painting. In 1949 he began to design his own home. What happened during this lapse of time? The answer is simple: O'Gorman felt disillusioned with functional architecture.

**Figure 3.9**
The outside of O'Gorman's house where pre-Columbian symbolism stands out from the natural polychromatic effect of the stones.

**Figure 3.10**
Juan O'Gorman in
his home, 1951.

Juan O'Gorman's home was built in 1951 in
the outskirts of Mexico City. He took the
topographical structure of the place very much
into account. It was built in a part of Mexico City
called Pedregal de San Angel, which looks like: '**a
rocky sea of lava formed by the eruptions of
(two volcanoes) the Ajusco and the Xitle.
When the lava cooled, it hardened into curved
waves held up by varied levels of terrain**',
according to Antonio Luna Arroyo.[15] This is
where O'Gorman, more than building, embedded
his project under a real rocky ledge that actually
became the roof for his home.

O'Gorman wanted cultural integration with
the geographical location, and beginning with
universal humanism, he wished not only to
restore pre-Columbian tradition but to modernise
it. O'Gorman managed to accomplish this by
using mosaics with aboriginal symbols to
decorate the outside walls of his house and by
creating a structure shaped like a pyramid. This
effort, in the ironic words of Raquel Tibol, came
to be called 'Indigenous Neo-Baroque.'

It seems opportune to mention the Olympic
Stadium at University City in Mexico City. It is
located relatively close to O'Gorman's house and
is in front of the university library which he
designed. The original plan was similar to a
stadium in the United States, but when
excavation was begun on the volcanic rock, a
sort of crater was discovered. Juan O'Gorman
explains the design of architect Pérez Palacios:
'**Owing to the fact that the Stadium at
University City was not completed according
to the original plans, an important example of
organic architecture was created. The filling
of packed dirt, lined with volcanic rock taken
from the site where it was originally built,
constitutes the solid wall on the top part of
the bleachers (series of steps), connects and
harmonises the architecture with the rocky
landscape of Pedregal, and gives a pyramidal
aspect to the place implying continuation or,
even better, a modernisation of pre-Hispanic
tradition. It could be said that this is the only
instance in the world where organic
architecture has been produced by chance;
the cost of the building procedure determined
its architecture.**'[16]

**Figure 3.11**
University City
Stadium, National
University, Mexico
City. Perez Palacios,
1952.

Juan O'Gorman also commented: '**The people of Mexico using newspapers stuck together with homemade paste, the cheapest clay they could find..., and a cheap lead pencil often put together with a stone hung from a hemp cord make their things, their toys, their wonderful Judases at Easter time, and the domestic tools that they need... Pablo Picasso's ceramics could hardly be distinguished among the multicoloured earthenware casserole dishes and pots that can be purchased for two pesos in any market in Mexico. But our architects do not want to see the truth of the situation and persist in a boring, imported architecture that turns out to be faded and expensive. They refuse to turn their eyes to the earth they walk on, the earth that sustains them, and they keep on yearning for what they call 'pure art', very cultured and very chic, even though disdained in Paris and in New York, and obstinately copy any architecture as long as it is in style at the moment.**'[17]

Brief sketches follow of some of the architects who, in one way or another, have approached the contemporary organic school of thought, albeit in a more intellectually flirtatious way. These architects, together with Niemeyer, Bruce Goff, Jörn Utzon, Paolo Soleri, Jacques Cöell, Antti Lovag, Pascal Haussman, Daniel Grataloup, and many others, have produced their work principally in the second half of the twentieth century. Not all the architects who should be on this list are here, however, nor are all those here truly organic architects.

**Figure 3.12**
The Astrophysics Institute in Potsdam, eastern Germany, also known as the 'Einstein Tower.' Erich Mendelsohn, 1920–1924.

## Erich Mendelsohn: Fusing the Matter

Considered by many to be the first and almost prophetic antithesis of boxy architecture, the Einstein Tower was constructed 34 years before Le Corbusier's Ronchamp Chapel.

Mendelsohn explained that through this work he was trying to raise '**a monument to the mystique that surrounded Einstein's universe.**'[18] This affirmation may seem paradoxical if we see it from the following perspective: Einstein's theory of physics came to relativise the world, to split it like an atom, while the merit of Mendelsohn and his tower is, according to Giuló Dorfles, to have developed '**a three-dimensional vision of the space in which the constant integration between the plan and the construction is the result of the unitary concept of the building conceived as a monolithic system**',[19] only fused together. In other words, the Einstein Tower is a monument to the disintegration of matter integrated into matter.

Mendelsohn had originally proposed creating his plastic work of architecture with poured concrete, but materials for the casting were so scarce after the First World War that he had to resort to building with masonry rubble and modelling it with plaster.

## Le Corbusier: the Return of Dionysius

Charles Édouard Jeanneret Gris was born in the Chaux-de-Fonds, Switzerland in 1887. Years later this rebellious man used the pseudonym Le Corbusier.

Le Corbusier (1887–1965) began his career by learning engraving in the School of Arts and Crafts in the city of his birth. After travelling through different countries and immersing himself in the spirit of European vernacular architecture, he settled down in what would become his second homeland, France. Once in Paris the obvious thing to do at that time would have been to enter the School of Fine Arts, but instead he turned to the workshop of Auguste Perret, where he learned how to use reinforced concrete which he would later mould as if it were clay. During the First World War he returned to Switzerland where he dedicated himself to teaching.

It is said that Le Corbusier, a curious child, found the dried remains of a crab when walking along the beach on Long Island, New York. Years later, while designing the Chapel at Notre Dame du Haut, Ronchamp, the crab was always there on his drawing board.

Le Corbusier's architectural ideas could be synthesised in the chapel at Ronchamp. Without doubt, it was there that he arrived at the concepts with which he theorised and played.

He reunited painting, sculpture and architecture – three arts that naturally belong together. In this sense it may be defined as three-dimensional, rather than one-dimensional, organic architecture. Robert Forneau Jordan referred to Notre Dame du Haut as the most three-dimensional object ever conceived and built. It is an architectural sculpture which one can enter, walk through, meditate in, and enjoy. Located at the top of a hill, the chapel not only becomes part of the existing environment – the

walls follow the natural slope from the top of the hill – but is itself built like a living organism. The asymmetry, the curved wall, and the playful support of light make Notre Dame du Haut rise into the air like a representative of anti-rationalistic architecture.

In addition to this, Le Corbusier turned his back on technological idealism and the aesthetics of a planned project, emphasising free creativity. Le Corbusier managed to do this by returning to the principles of vernacular architecture and by directing his feelings towards anonymity, returning to the heart of the matter and relegating the brain somewhat. In other words he invoked the Dionysian spirit of art in order to be able to create what Stephen Garden called musical architecture.

Notre Dame du Haut is, above all, a religious temple and as such fulfils its function. Its wall, 3 metres thick, provides total isolation. Silence is heard from the altar to the confessionals. The light, concentrated and direct, crosses the space like divine breath. The sensation of serenity overcomes the visitor, even the non-believer, and makes one breathe easily and tranquilly.

It is important to point out Le Corbusier's respect for French cultural tradition. The previous chapel built on this site had been bombed and all but destroyed during the Second World War. Le Corbusier added the remains of this earlier chapel to his own building materials and retained the image of the original patron saint at the main altar.

**Figure 3.15**
The interior of the chapel in Ronchamp. © Photo Researchers Inc./Eric Shings.

## Alvar Aalto: from Necessity to Spontaneous Design

Alvar Aalto (1898–1976), the Finnish architect and designer, integrated his materials, the structure itself, and psychology into most of his designs. Some element that is the product of the building's function usually stands out. Instead of boxing it inside a symmetrical, rigid wrapping, he liberated it, allowing his imagination to run free. Alvar Aalto himself described his architecture as becoming more rational than international architecture. The structures he built in Finland in particular incorporated mixed materials such as timber, brick and copper thus blending his designs into the landscape.

Lamps and furniture were integral to his designs: '**painting and sculpture are part of my working method. Consequently I do not like to see them separated. For me... they are branches from the same tree, and architecture is the trunk.**'[20]

For Aalto, architecture was a synthetic phenomenon that embraced nearly every human activity, a combination of brilliant analysis and profound intuition. Aalto made this comment: '**Generally the number of demands and problems hinder us and make it difficult to get a basic idea... When this happens, I instinctively do the following in many cases: I forget all about the major part of the problem for a little while, and as soon as I feel that the conditions are involved with my unconscious, I take up the whole job again and carry out the process in my subconscious, making use of all the accumulated material and gradually get to the main idea, a sort of universal essence which helps me harmonise elemental conflict.**'[21] This logical, beautiful formula, however, is not always one that will help other architects obtain good results.

**Figure 3.16**
Ville Carre. Bazoches-sur-Guyonne (France) 1956-1959. Aalto. © Architectural Association, M. Quantriu.

**Figure 3.17**
A crystal vase. Alvar
Aalto, 1973.

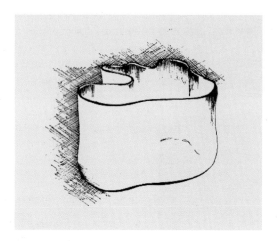

**Figure 3.18**
The undulating form
of the Bakerhouse
dormitory at M.I.T.,
Cambridge,
Massachusetts, USA.
Completed 1949.

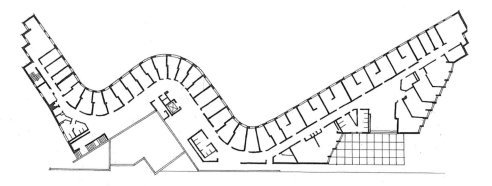

### Enrique Castañeda Tamborrel: Architecture as an Integrated Whole

After winning the contest for the Mount Olympus Housing Project in Hollywood, California, USA, Castañeda Tamborrel stated that: '**The direct material result, or the result produced by the material, obeys an ecstatic sensibility while at the same time satisfying an obvious aesthetic need in harmony with my own sensitivity.**'[22]

Reinforced concrete and plastic materials allow the architect to free himself from a series of canons. If, on top of that, he manages to express the whole idea clearly and bring together the isolated elements into one common whole, he will succeed in achieving the organic structural character of his work.

In the case of social housing which obviously suggests mass-production or prefabrication with a minimum number of elements, Enrique Castañeda Tamborrel's organic vision of an integrated whole was equally important to the cost of the project and to the time taken to construct it. Castañeda Tamborrel concludes by saying, '**The principal aim consisted in the achievement of a unique, indivisible whole constituted by just one material, and this whole gives the impression of being an enormous, solid block.**'[23]

**Figure 3.19**
Housing project:
winner of the Mount
Olympus residential
competition,
Hollywood, California,
USA. Enrique
Castañeda
Tamborrel, 1964.

**Figure 3.20**
Interior view of the church in Atlántida, Uruguay.

**Figure 3.21**
Exterior view of the church in Atlántida, Uruguay.

In order to achieve rhythm and structural unity in the design of the campanile and its apertures, Dieste constructed horizontal beams to run only part of the way round the circumference of the tower. An alternative solution would have been to make a continuous ring out of each of the beams. However, Dieste discovered that this method would have unbalanced the coherence and structural unity of the tower.

## Eladio Dieste: From Hard Materials to Soft Architecture

We do not know if this ingenious Uruguayan, together with the Columbian, Rogelio Salmona and the Mexican, Carlos Mijares, play with bricks in order to build or build in order to play. One example is the small church at the beach resort of Atlántida, Uruguay where, with great humility, Dieste presents an architectural poem created from brick in which undulating lateral walls support the roof – a chiaroscuro scheme involving shape, space, and texture.

## Rogelio Salmona: Sculptural Brick

Salmona's work reveals his obvious preoccupation for the surroundings and respect for environmental conditions. While helping to improve the quality of urban life Salmona also makes good use of the building techniques of his own country, Columbia, particularly in the use of brick.

The centre-piece of his work, a group of buildings known as 'Park Towers' (Torres del Parque), makes his architectural and landscape work stand out by integrating the group of buildings with the bull-ring and having the silhouette of the mountains that surround Bogotá as a background.

In spite of its magnitude, the group of buildings does not lose its human scale thanks to the use of mass based on the dynamic, suggestive curves of the terraces and balconies, and the treatment of outside areas as a continuation of the brick 'skin' of the buildings themselves. All this makes it possible for Park Towers to offer new and different visual effects, generating interplay of unexpected and surprising light and shadow, resulting from its brick-covered reliefs.

## Carlos Mijares: Architectural Basketwork

Arches, vaults, fan tracery vaulting, squinch arches, and skylights made of brick constitute the architectural elements with which Carlos Mijares, a Mexican architect, has created works of great, expressive richness. He experiments with new and different ways of designing, in which time and the participation of the craftsmen involved play a central role, so much so that the blueprints turn out to be useless. This gives rise to a process in which the elements acquire dimensions, shapes, textures, and suitable places under one principal, governing idea.

The use of naked brick in walls is characteristic of his work. Rather than being limited to the traditional role, they are introduced into the space and become arches, elements, and plaques, the texture of which creates a rhythmic weave of rows and interrelations, producing a pattern of brick similar to basketwork.

In buildings like the chapels in Ciudad Hidalgo and Jungapeo, his work recovers transcendent humanistic values and incorporates them into the language of contemporary architecture, thereby capturing in the spaces the soul of the people it represents, at once traditional and modern.

**Figure 3.22**
View of Park Towers, Bogotá, Columbia. Rogelio Salmona, 1964–1970.

**Figure 3.23**
Interior detail of the chapel at the cemetery in Jungapeo, Michoacán, Mexico. Carlos Mijares, 1982–1986.

### Hundertwasser: Co-existence with Nature

Hundertwasser approached architecture as an artist and an environmental activist. The Hundertwasser House in Vienna (see Figure 3.24) was one of his first commissions. Handed over to its tenants in 1986, this was a public housing project, designed in reaction to a multitude of monotonous, grey, boxlike municipal apartments.

His loathing of straight lines and right angles partially stemmed from a philosophical parallel with the rigidity of dictatorships and fascist regimes, both of which stifled creativity and individuality, and were disharmonious with the natural world.

Trees emerge from the windows of the Vienna house, and plants crowd the several terrace gardens. Not only did Hundertwasser bring the tenants closer to nature, he designed the foliage as a contribution to the life of the building, providing shade from the sun, shelter from the wind, and a filter for water. Careful thought went into the choice of trees and shrubs, to ensure year-round flora. These are an integral part of the building, which along with the multitude of colours in the façade, allow the architecture to vary and develop with time and the seasons.

Hundertwasser's work is characterised by diversity of colour, use of uneven, irregular and curved surfaces, and the integration of plantlife. His vision was of cities invisible from the air, made indistinguishable from forests and meadows by the replanting of roofs.

**Figure 3.24**
House façade ©
Architectural
Association/Hazel
Cook.

6 Colourfulness, variety and diversity are by all means better than the grey, the average grey... 9

Hundertwasser[24]

6 Why can an individual not live up to himself as a flower does? 9

Hundertwasser[25]

**Figure 3.25**
(a and b – next page) Hungarian Pavilion © John Edward Linden.

## Makovecz: Buildings with Soul

The name of Imre Makovecz is synonymous with the organic movement in twentieth century Hungarian architecture.

His international reputation was made by the impressive seven-towered Hungarian Pavilion, designed for the 1992 World Exposition in Seville (see Figure 3.25). This timber construction demonstrates the characteristically extensive use of organic materials in Makovecz's work.

Makovecz's extensive magnification of natural icons, such as the tulip and the falcon, is rooted in the symbolism of Hungarian folk traditions and in a mythological outlook linking past, present and future. His buildings are yet more heavily laden with anthropomorphic elements, inspired by the philosophies of Goethe and Rudolf Steiner. His architectural organisms are alive, possessing a soul or spirit that communicates with the community and unites it in social richness.

The instinctively assymetrical shapes inherent in his designs follow the shapes of nature, but also try to capture a complex spirit of individuality and personality, so that society draws inspiration from the individual who defies geometrical and theoretical convention.

❝Trees are the most complete representation of life. Branches are supernatural aspirations and roots represent the mysterious unconscious❞

Makovecz[26]

❝I believe that the original intention of our architecture was to create an architectural connection between the sky and the earth, a connection which enlightens and expresses man's movement and position, to create a magic, weaving an invisible spell on its surroundings❞

Makovecz[27]

(b)

**Figure 3.26**
(a–d) (a on previous page and d on the next page). Railway station at the airport, Lyon, France, by Santiago Calatrava. © John Edward Linden; (c) cross section. Cathedral of St. John the Divine, New York City, USA. Santiago Calatrava, 1991.

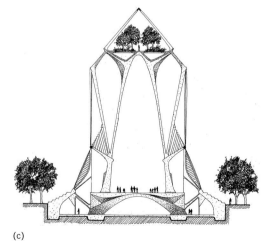

(c)

**Opposite** Inside the Hungarian Pavilion. © John Edward Linden.

## Santiago Calatrava: the Art of Possibilities

As the author of an architecture that is in keeping with technological possibilities, where structure constitutes a balance between efficient scientific criteria and harmonious forms, Calatrava achieves the fusion of sculpture, architecture and engineering, showing his knowledge of each one of these.

The beautiful, dynamic shapes of his creations are the result of the formal expression of the forces in them – experiments with the basic laws of statics in which a section of the plan is just as important as the whole design.

Calatrava's language is organic, not because he copies natural shapes but because he applies the same structural solutions adopted by nature. As he himself says, '**working with isostatic structures almost inevitably takes you into the schematic diagrams of nature.**'[28]

The skilful use of traditional materials is characteristic of his work: steel, concrete, glass, wood, stone, and aluminium are used in such a way that he obtains the best structural qualities each has to offer.

Among his architectural works, the winning design in the contest to finish the north and south transepts of the Cathedral of St John the Divine in New York City, USA, is the most outstanding. His plans introduced a new element: a refuge for humans. This meant that he needed to integrate solar and electronic technology for food production, water purification, and the

recycling of wastes, among other requirements, in his architectural design.

Calatrava's design was innovative: he placed the refuge immediately underneath the steel and glass roof. Using the image of a tree as the basic element of the composition – an image that reminds one of the shapes used by Gaudí in the temple of La Sagrada Familia – he offers a new interpretation of the structural system of the building and at the same time, maintains the archetypal shape of the cathedral.

## Eugene Tsui: Communion with Nature

Through partnership between nature and humanity, Eugene Tsui advocates a wholly new outlook and philosophy of innovative architecture, based upon the scientific study of nature as a catalyst for the practical needs and spiritual vision of the twenty-first century individual. Tsui's artistic originality combined with the profound intelligence of nature's structures and processes results in spectacular buildings that are not merely catchy flamboyance. His buildings make artistic, functional and ecological sense.

Building in harmony with the surrounding natural environment, Tsui specifically uses non-toxic materials and utilises, preserves and enhances local ecosystems, as well as using solar and wind power, constructed wetlands and existing water sources to create structures that are self-sufficient in energy needs. His motivations go further than environmental concerns – Tsui looks to nature '**...for solutions to our moral, architectural and spiritual evolution. By studying the profound lessons of nature – committing ourselves to this life long study –**

**we can learn how to live without destroying the earth and each other**'[29].

Rejecting the shiny, fragmented, chaotic dissonance of present architectural trends and the boxy sameness of past traditional styles, Tsui moves away from an industrial, computer driven, image oriented architecture in a philosophical response to the numbing and alienating effect past architecture has had on a person's soul. By delving into the unknown and applying the interdisciplinary knowledge of engineering, biology, zoology, ecology, materials sciences and art, a new path of creativity, passion and the artistry of humankind is unleashed.

Tsui's architecture directly applies nature's lessons. The Tsui Residence (see Figure 3.28a–c), billed as the world's safest house, is based upon the incredibly strong structure of the microscopic Tardigrade and its subsurface solar heating system was conceived from the bone and capillary design of dinosaurs. The house features a hidden drainage system that prevents flooding and a south-facing 'eyeball' window that magnifies winter sunlight absorbed by interior walls for natural heating. Its aerodynamic elliptical shape and rough-textured walls help prevent fire carried by breeze by directing wind away from the house. The house uses a styrene and concrete block system that is termite-proof and extremely sound absorbent (50 decibels). Its hemispherical windows allow 180 degree views and are 200 times stronger than flat glass.

Structures that move and respond to the climate have been designed by Tsui, as a form of living, or 'evolutionary' architecture. An example is the Reyes Residence (see Figure 3.27a–c) – the beautiful wing structures, inspired by the dragonfly, can be opened and closed with the turn of a crank, allowing manual control of hot

> ❛I do not look to nature as inspiration merely to mimic its forms as other architects have done. I am concerned with the profound intelligence of nature, the how's and why's of its designs and living processes, to understand the very mind of nature and the universe to free the heart and mind of man ❜
>
> Eugene Tsui, personal quote, 2003.

**Figure 3.28**
(a–c) The Tsui
Residence © Eugene
Tsui.

(a)

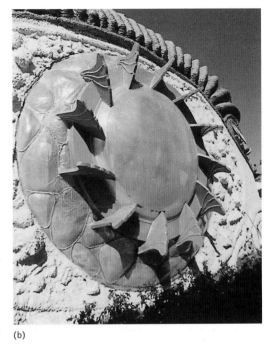

(b)

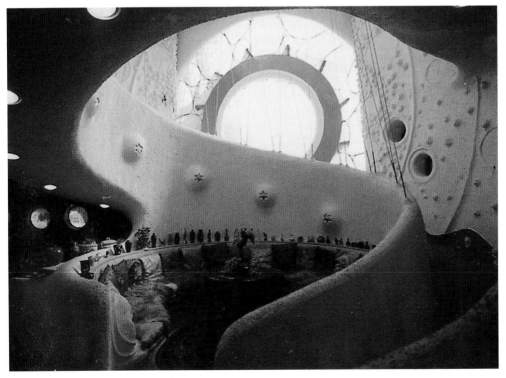

(d)

(a)

and cool air which controls the temperature and humidity of the house and affords direct views of the sky and stars. It's truncated conical design makes it very stable and resistant to earthquakes. This house is perhaps the first instance in modern architecture of moving parts as crucial features in a building which adapt to the changing needs of the climate and the inhabitants. An example of Tsui's vision of architecture as a kind of living organism for the functional and spiritual benefit of humans.

(b)

**Figure 3.27**
(a–c) The Reyes Residence © Eugene Tsui.

# The search for space

Today, with the exception of socio-economic absurdities and the equally grotesque injustices prevalent in our world, humans have more than enough technological ability to build highly functional housing. Contemporary technology gives us the tools and the methods to create internal spaces at will – we are able to modify temperature, humidity and light. Nevertheless, as Udo Kultermann pointed out, only when we really know how we want to live and what we expect of our homes, will we truly know our goals.

## Physical and Psychological Well-being

It is ironic that before building a zoo, the natural conditions in which each species lives and its behaviour in the wild are studied in order to design an appropriate artificial space for captivity. The irony lies in the fact that more is known about the spatial behaviour of animals than about that of human beings. In fact, most of the recent studies of spatial anthropology find their immediate antecedent in the zoo.

Each animal species requires a specific living space and each animal demands a certain amount of individual space, so much so that the need to maintain it often leads to violence. Looking at the situation from this angle, Forrest Wilson questioned whether it is even possible for human beings to adjust themselves to spatial conditions that promote indiscriminate mingling.

❛Organic architecture is the artistic manifestation that directly relates to the geography and history of the site built on❜

Juan O'Gorman

Krech carried out a very significant experiment that consisted of putting two groups of rats in diametrically opposed conditions. With the first group, he attempted to reproduce the conditions in ghettos and poor New York neighbourhoods as closely as possible: he gave them an overload of sensory stimuli, a poor and unvaried diet, very little natural light, and so on. The second group was raised in a different atmosphere with colours, textures, soft music... It is easy to anticipate the results: those in the second group had greater learning aptitudes, faster mental development, greater flexibility and adaptability to new stimuli, and markedly superior memories. '**The dissection demonstrated that the cerebral cortex of these rats was larger, heavier, and had more convolutions**',[30] stated Victor Papanek in his report.

*Let us attempt to reconstruct the working day of a typical inhabitant of any western city. At six o'clock in the morning, a clamorous alarm clock jerks him out of his sleep; at seven, along with dozens of other individuals like himself, he waits for a bus. When at last it arrives, he manages with a lot of luck and much audacity to board it. It would be absurd to discuss individual space inside the bus; the Aristotelian law of the impenetrability of matter is almost proven incorrect. People pile on and beyond a certain point all are affected by the smallest movement. Getting off the bus and entering the underground is an even more extreme experience. Once in the office, the man is confronted by the sound of computers, radios, confused voices, an aeroplane flying overhead, a coffee pot coming to the boil, telephones that never seem to stop ringing, and on and on. On his way home, he faces the same difficulties all over again. Our man has spent eight hours in an office and a couple more inside buses and underground trains. Now, he unlocks his front door and ...*

The above demonstrates that architecture should not only provide us with a physical service, a place where our basic physiological needs are supplied, but just as importantly, it should contribute to the mental well-being of inhabitants. The physiological needs of human beings are the same world over, the same now as they were thousands of years ago: humans need room to cook, rest, sleep, wash, bathe, and relieve themselves of waste.

Psychological needs, although they have essential and relatively universal characteristics, vary from one culture to another, from one social class to another, and from one individual to another.

Reine Mehl has stated the fundamental purposes of architecture in the following terms: '**Man has always sought to satisfy two basic needs by building a shelter: protection from the elements and an ambience that is favorable to carrying out human endeavours.**'[31] In order to comply satisfactorily with the first of these objectives, the architect must know about the ecology of the place where the building is to be constructed, the biology of the user, and a certain amount of physics. In order to satisfy the psychological needs of the human being, on the other hand, a deep knowledge of the individual psyche of the future inhabitant as well as the cultural cosmovision of his environment are necessary. The combination of these two factors will result in an appropriate, comfortable dwelling.

Balancing these factors implies, in the first place, that when we speak of physical and psychological well-being, we understand them as a unity, as an inseparable whole.

Reine Mehl draws attention to some aspects which should be considered: '**Low barometric pressure can produce reluctance, restlessness, and lack of concentration, and even make an adult feel upset or angry and a child feel irritable. Police records in large cities indicate that more acts of violence are committed, and this includes suicide, when barometric pressure goes down to less than 30 inches of mercury.**'[32] By contrast, a person's well-being is almost guaranteed if he lives in a place that provides suitable ambient conditions, and that, precisely, is the duty of architecture.

When an architect designs a structure to be inhabited, he must consider all the human senses. In contemporary western culture most information about the external world comes through the eyes. So much importance is given to visual observation that other senses are often relegated to second place, even to the extent of constructing buildings designed only to impress from the outside with little consideration for what is fundamentally most important: the needs of those who live there. Housing should not only be pleasing to look at, but it should also appeal to all the other senses even if it is at a subconscious level.

Building contractors need to handle colour and shape, it is true, but smell, sound, light, and texture, are all important. Troglodyte dwellings were pleasant even to touch.

It is crucial that architecture combines the beautiful, the useful, and the comfortable: a dwelling should please, refresh and revive. Wright was always convinced that a beautiful building helps people resolve their conflicts in life – that a harmonious house has a tranquillising effect. When he designed something, he did it with the desire to liberate, to give a feeling of joy, not of oppression.

The twenty-first century human will need to regain the mental and spiritual tranquillity lost over recent generations of urban life; the only way to achieve this is to modify the surroundings, making them less oppressive and more natural.

## The Curve

People have certain instincts that make them feel the loss of natural shapes. Heinz Rasch explains: **'The circle, which we will use as an archetype, belongs to our earliest impressions: the moon, the sun, the eyes, the mouth, an apple, a ball. Cezanne remarked that one could reduce everything he sees to three circular shapes: the sphere, the cone, and the cylinder....'** Our perception works so that **'when one finds himself in a complex optical situation, he seeks the most suitable form of unity or the least confused relationships in the environment. Goethe observed that the post-image of a clear picture may suddenly become round and acquire a circular shape...'**[33]

In primitive cultures, curvilinear forms appear as constant symbols of cosmogony. The serpent in Central-American cultures represents a basic dynamic of life; the cave in troglodyte cultures and the shell in thalassic cultures symbolises the womb. The human being, relating to nature, develops cultural symbolisms that reflect similar needs.

According to the universal laws of physics, movement tends to produce curved or spherical forms. There are many examples: electrons; structures eroded by air or water such as stones in rivers and stalactites; meteorites; drops of water; planets. The fastest moving living beings become curved. This can be explained by the fact that all bodies that develop a certain velocity tend to have small surfaces to avoid friction. The sphere is the geometrical form that possesses less perimeter surface in relation to volume; it has maximum internal space with a minimum of external surface.

Everything moves, changes, and evolves. Any movement in any part of the human organism, for instance, causes a reaction in the rest of the body. Thus, when someone moves through different spaces, they will always have a reaction in their feelings and senses.

*Imagine a swallow flying in an absolutely straight line, or a fly following a grid of squares, or the moon turning around the Earth in a perfect square. If you can do that, then you have quite an imagination. Now picture a mountain, replete with trees and fauna. Add a wide, flowing river to that scene... Imagine the river flowing rapidly down a rectilinear riverbed turning at right angles. It's almost impossible, isn't it?*

In nature the maxim of movement is found in the curved line – the trajectory of a point moving between two places by a route, not the shortest distance between the two positions. Curves are the product of variable, complementary forces. Using rivers as an example: '**The Po River, the Tiber River, or any other river, is born close to the top of a mountain and in two seconds is already a torrent. It descends the mountain by a valley, and always running towards the lowest places of the area, it slides over small slopes, grows in the great valleys, creates a serpentine path across uneven, rough terrain, and heads directly for the plains. A river has a natural, organic shape**',[34] comments Bruno Munari.

Nevertheless, we must be cautious here. Phrases like 'unpredictable natural shapes' or 'unexpected direction of the riverbed' could be misinterpreted. The appearance of something is not its essence: if nature developed unreasonably, the world simply would not work.

On the contrary, curved lines have a reason for being. Every natural movement is expressed in curves, and observing constellations, the movements of celestial bodies, the rising and setting of the sun, the wind that blows, or the clouds, proves this.

All natural products are unique and cannot be duplicated. Consider this, taken from the catalogue of the first Paris exposition of the Facchetti studio on rue de Lille (January, 1954):

*'I have a bicycle. Paris is large. I want to say: The lines drawn by my bicycle through the streets of Paris are extraordinary. My curved lines are only as incredible as the other lines that I cross, laid down by people and their vehicles. I can use my bicycle wheels like a paintbrush as I move along, and I am happy to be in contact and in harmony with the other lines. These lines that make me weary when I make them are more beautiful, more genuine, and more justified than those I could draw on paper. I would not be surprised if the lines I make with my feet on the paved surface on the way to the museum are more important than the lines I will find hanging on the walls.*[35]

Nature evolves out of certain rhythms and cyclical patterns which are impossible to represent with absolute breaks. If walking is essentially a rhythmic process composed of a discontinuous succession of steps, the path should not be inflexible or homogeneous.

**Figure 3.29**
Animals with aerodynamic and hydrodynamic forms that move rapidly in air, on land, and in water.

**Figure 3.30**
In the Shinsen Kyo moss garden at the MOA Museum of Fine Arts in Hakone, Japan. © Photograph courtesy of the MOA Museum of Fine Art.

The path follows the natural slope of the land, making walking through it

an adventure and not a mere necessity

In Central Park in New York City, the paths set at right angles that link the museums disappear when it snows. The elegant shapes of slaloms appear in their place. The word *slalom* comes from Norwegian and describes the curves traced by a skier on the snow. Scott correctly points out that '**in design, the shortest distance between two points is not a straight line but a slalom.**'[36] Scott describes slaloms as curves with acceleration and deceleration that represent a trajectory controlled by humans. The curves made by the movement of a car or bicycle on flat surfaces are defined as two-dimensional slaloms. Those paths followed by mountaineers or aeroplanes that rise and fall, like those of skiers, are called slaloms of a third order.

Once a well-known architect built a complex of large office buildings in an empty field. When the construction was finished, the landscapers consulted him on how he wanted the grass turfs and plants to be laid out. 'Not yet,' answered the architect. 'Just plant grass over the entire area between the buildings.' These instructions were followed and by the end of the summer, the grass had been marked by paths going from one building to another or from the buildings to the outside. These paths followed the most efficient line between one point and another creating comfortable curves instead of right angles, and had the correct width for the flow of pedestrian traffic. During the autumn the architect designed the permanent walkways based on these paths. Not only did he achieve beautiful walkways but these paths also corresponded exactly to the needs of the users. Besides, it was never necessary to put up any warning signs such as 'Please Do Not Walk On the Grass.'

When analysing the layout of city streets, you can see that architects and city planners manipulate us as though we were mechanical entities. On the other hand, some designs such as musical instruments continue to use the curve as their essential shape. Other manual tools, like kitchen appliances, are also designed according to their ergonomic function.

**Figure 3.31**
The French horn is an example of how the curve continues to be used in the design of musical instruments.

### The Organic

At the beginning of the eighteenth century, people began to use the terms 'organism' and 'organisation' to describe a harmonious combination of parts. The word 'organic', that comes from biology, means organisation as it is related to the animal and plant kingdoms, and was applied for the first time to architecture in Paris, in 1863.

Although there are some exceptions, organic architecture is based on the experience and independence of Euclidean geometry. For Frank Lloyd Wright: **'the word organic in architecture denotes not only what can be hung in a butcher shop, carried on two feet, or cultivated in a field. The word organic also refers to the entity, and perhaps it would be better to use the word integral or intrinsic. As it was originally used in architecture, organic means a part of the whole and all of the part'**.[38]

The architectural whole is perceived as an absolute, and each part is created and put in exactly the right place to obtain the unity desired. Not everything is the sum of its parts but rather the integration of each one of the parts. Aristotle called this concept **'one sole and indivisible principle of unity'**[39] which no longer represented a metaphysical principle but a biological fact. A live animal (and this includes humans) is an integral, indivisible whole – not one part can be changed without affecting another, and there is no clear division between the head and the body, the muscle and the tendon, the fibre and the bone.

The first of Cuvier's two well-known anatomical rules is the correlation of all parts, which shows that: **'all the organs of an animal form one system in which each part is united with all others, acting on and reacting with each other.'**[40] Viollet Le Duc commented: **'From the chance that contemplation of a leaf can lead to deductions about the whole plant, and the whole animal can be deduced by contemplation of a bone, so architectural parts can be deduced from a section and the whole monument from the architectural parts.'**[41] The same thing happens when a building and its environment constitute an integrated whole: **'site, building, furniture, decoration, trees, plants; everything becomes one... This is what posterity will later call organic architecture'**,[42] Frank Lloyd Wright would say.

Cuvier's second rule is the subordination of characteristic features: some of the organs or systems of the body have more functional significance than others, ordering themselves according to importance. The organs or principle elements form a basis for integration of the rest. In architecture, there are spaces that govern the composition as a whole, others that complement the essentials. Alvar Aalto conceived structure as an organism, while rational architecture perceives it as a mechanism. The difference is clear: the latter seeks buildings that work, while the former seeks buildings with life.

❝Bomarza's wonderful, fanciful architecture close to Viterbo should be remembered. The rooms of the park keepers are giant heads: the architect decided that the mouth should be the front door and the eyes should be the windows. There you have an example of imagination, poetry, architecture, and painting joined together❞

Juan O'Gorman[37]

This has nothing to do with copying nature. Up to now nothing has been copied perfectly although we can consider and take natural principles into account. Just as one can feel the stresses in the embedment of a beam with a column, so one can enter a Gothic cathedral and comprehend the configuration of the building as a whole and its stresses. In the same way, one can learn to sense the internal detail of forms found in nature. Deep submersion in the process of organic growth in architecture produces shapes that remind us of those in nature.

Organic architecture looks for three integral aspects: the functional, which implies the process and mode of life; the constructive, which includes materials and technology; and the aesthetic, where the ideological-emotional structure is located. What we call mercantile architecture only considers the first two aspects, and society wastes resources to produce physical and emotional debris. When aesthetics form the only objective in a building, something called 'formalism' appears, a deformation of the architectural image.

For O'Gorman: '**organic architecture is the artistic manifestation that directly relates to the geography and history of the site built on. Architecture then becomes the means of creating harmony between man and the earth, reflecting the earth and the colour of the environment where the building is constructed.**'[43] In other words, organic architecture is characterised mainly by taking into account the geographic environment, the human being, and his cultural identity.

## Human Space

In antiquity, words had vibrations that made one feel the deep significance of things. The Sanskrit words for house were *skauti* (meaning to hide oneself) and *kuahra* (which actually meant house). Over the years, these words were disseminated and translated into most of the languages of Europe and the Middle East. In ancient Persian, the word was *keuto* (to hide oneself); in Greek it was *kutos* (hollow); in Latin it was *scutum* (shelter, safety, protection).

A home is like a second skin that protects us from danger. It is a magical space in which theoretically, fear is left outside. It is a refuge that welcomes us day after day.

To improve the human dwelling two elements need to be integrated, the three-dimensional quality of space and the fourth dimension, time. To do this means putting aside the limitations of a two-dimensional blueprint and using a model instead. Time, place and rhythm of life must all be considered. It is important to remember that the spatial experience of anyone living in the house will vary depending on where they are, and as they move around it will continually change. Keeping this in mind, the architect can project, beyond real dimensions, a continuous space based on spatial experience. The fourth dimension is the time that person spends moving about and capturing this changing vision. Each space needs to be designed both to be seen and to be lived in. Leonardo Ricci wrote: '**that architecture needed to be freed from rigid concepts of space, moving toward those concepts in which it could flow freely.**'[44]

Antoni Gaudí's Güell Park, Le Corbusier's Ronchamp Chapel, the Pavilion of Finland, or the *Via XX* by Settembre in Roma, are all examples of how daring architects of our time have explored creative paths in search of a concept of space that evaluates the dynamic in architecture. Architecture that neglects time and space creates merely things, not homes.

**Figure 3.32**
'Endless House' designed by Frederick Kiesler, 1929.

The 'Endless House' of Frederick Kiesler may be the building that pays most attention to the ideal of architectural dynamism. Kiesler explains: **'The dimensions and the arrangement... are determined by the different activities and personal experiences of those who inhabit it. Its free form comes from the fact that each section of the house can be opened and closed in a continuous, unique space.'**[45] Each part of the home involves a different shape depending on the inhabitant and his lifestyle. Also: **'the shape and final model of the house are determined by the usual measurements of height, width, and depth required for the necessary activities of eating, sleeping, walking, and working. The well-defined functional areas can be opened or closed to the other areas thereby creating a continuous space'**,[46] points out Ken Kern. The product of these characteristics centres its basic foundations on natural principles, essentially on the kinetics of curved shapes.

The inspiration of architectural space through observing nature leads to the concept of the dwelling-organism. In the 1950s the American, Sanford Hauser **'imagined a beautiful design of a house by the beach. His observation of the waves and small, round pebbles suggested the shape of the house to him'**,[47] writes Michael Ragon in his book *Where Shall We Live Tomorrow?* From here on, egg-shaped constructions followed one after another; for example, the one that Pascal Hauserman built with his own money, and continuing on to Herman Finsterlin's concepts of the house-organism.

For Finsterlin, dwellings should be something more than a **'fantastic crystal gland.'** He believed that to enter a home, one should have the impression of being something more than an inhabitant who, in the end, is an intruder. Instead, one must **'feel like the internal inhabitant of an organism that moves from one organism to another like a symbiotic dweller that takes and receives from an enormous fossil womb.'**[48]

The principles of organic architecture have created the need for curved walls, ramps, caves, and habitable spaces (rooms) shaped like viscera, as opposed to flat walls, right angles, stairs, and self-contained rooms. Architecture should then compare its models with nature, not nature subordinate itself to designs. Some extreme cases can be found within this perspective. For some organic architects like Haring, the solution is found in Michelangelo's ideal: both talk of *finding* the shape instead of *giving* the shape, of *freeing* the shape instead of *imposing* it from the outside. In other words, their work consisted of helping things find their correct, appropriate form.

Architecture has neglected a taste for the everyday things of life, for the beauty of a home and the aesthetic pleasure that living in it bestows.

**Figure 3.33**
Design of a house on the beach by Sanford Hauser, 1956.

We already have the scientific and technological knowledge to develop a dignified daily lifestyle. We now have to build housing that provides not only physical, but also spiritual, protection.

In order to obtain harmonious human spaces, we should worry about something more than whether or not the heating system works, the doors open, the windows ventilate, or the roof is strong enough. A home should be something more than an appliance. The Apollonian spirit of harmony, order, and balance needs to be reconciled with the sensual, Dionysian spirit: the romantic ideal needs to be reconciled with the classic.

In this sense, André Bloc has been a great visionary. Arturo Pani explains that '**his sculptures present ample material modulations and audacious rhythm in the volumes, repeated curves, the interplay of voids and lights that penetrate, encircle, and filter through mysterious orifices.**'[49] In creating serene, balanced communication between the technical and the aesthetic, Bloc establishes the dialogue between the spiritual and the material.

The works of Barbara Hepworth and Henry Moore are excellent examples of hollow, empty spaces in architecture. Their work comes from the contemplation of the art of primitive cultures.

Describing his experience as a sculptor, Henry Moore says that as he penetrates deeper and deeper into the depth of the mass, he discovers a fascinating mystery in the joints between the inside and the outside, and when he illuminates the positive side of the mass from the outside, the reflection of its organic growth makes it even more monumental. The same is true of architecture; the holes for the windows can be pointed towards the sun, a breathtaking view, or located strategically for improved ventilation.

'**The doors and windows of a house are hollow spaces. The origin of the hollow of an urn moulded out of clay on a potter's wheel is the clay's absence**',[50] said Lao-Tse. Similarly, free, ecstatic spaces work in the same way '**to take the observer through a series of sequences which prove that the house is an organic whole and to design a model of rhythm, effects, and ordered sequences, finally coming to a climax.**'[51]

The integration of space is the result of rhythmic, natural designs. The rhythm in a home is achieved by means of a space which plays with the movements of expansion and contraction.

To speak of a comfortable building is to refer to free, continuous spaces that are, at the same time, private and closed. There is a strong relationship between the insides and the outsides, and close communion between the elements of the house. In a comfortable building, vital conflicts will be resolved within harmonious, serene spaces that simultaneously inspire liberating fantasies.

**Figure 3.34**
A sculpture by
Barbara Hepworth.

# The organic habitat

### The Original Idea

In my own work I have designed organic dwellings with the aim of creating spaces to suit our physical and psychological needs as well as our environment.

The idea was to look at the beginning of the human's origins in nature and the organic space throughout history to develop suitable living spaces. These spaces would be similar to the womb, an animal's lair, a troglodyte dwelling, an igloo... They would represent not a return to the past but rather a premeditated reconciliation.

From the very beginning, commercial, industrial, or conventional interests were put aside along with any inherited social or academic prejudices regarding architecture. This meant that constructional materials and technologies could be chosen without paying too much attention to their past or present use; instead, importance was placed on their ability to create continuous, ample, integral spaces which would liberate shapes. There would be strategically placed lights that would follow the natural rhythm of a human's movements. The spaces would have built-in, integrated furniture that would facilitate air circulation and take advantage of a great part of the constructed area.

At the same time, it was intended that the changing spaces inside would generate changing volumes on the outside – green 'dunes' that would invite rest and meditation, while children could slide down their slopes.

**❛Home and garden may now become one. In an organic structure, it is difficult to tell where the garden ends and the house begins or where the house ends and the garden begins ❜**

Reinhold Von Nostrand[52]

## Mouldable Materials

Perhaps the most difficult and troublesome part of the creative process is the path from the initial concept to the actual product, from the ideal to the end result, from what one has in mind to produce to what one can actually accomplish.

Certain building materials are associated with certain phases in the history of architecture. For example, the most common traditional materials are stone, wood and earth, which have been used since time immemorial. Adobe and wood remind us of vernacular constructions, whereas stone reminds us of medieval constructions. Later, materials such as oven-baked bricks and concrete, were used. Later still, steel was used – in the gently sweeping curves of the Eiffel Tower, for example – and so on. New techniques, materials and tools were introduced; they were sometimes obstacles, but sometimes leaps forward along the road of architectural development.

The invention and introduction of reinforced concrete in western architecture was an important step. Ferroconcrete (reinforced concrete) became a highly mouldable material that could be sculpted almost as easily as modelling clay. It is a material that opened new roads in design. Another malleable material that we are only now realising the full potential of is plastic and its derivatives. Such is the case with sprayed polyurethane plastic foam.

## The Organic House: Design and Outline of the House

Once the land had been obtained and the essential working practices laid down, the embryonic idea of the design began to resemble a peanut shell with two ample, oval, well-lit spaces connected by another low, narrow space in semi-darkness. This idea arose out of people's basic needs: a room to sleep in with a dressing-room and bath; and another less private room in which to socialise, sit, eat and cook. So it was finally decided that the house would have only two large rooms, and the initial, primitive concept of the house was now defined.

Next came a confrontation between the desire and the possibility. A topographical study was made of the terrain in which the locations of existing trees were particularly considered so they would be respected in the final plan.

Based on this study, a couple of clay models were made. One of them concentrated on the outside volumes and spaces, the other on the inside. Both were worked in parallel throughout the whole project.

A free hand was allowed in the process of design. This meant that trees could stay in place and orientation towards the south was maintained.

All of these factors almost involuntarily generated a mass reminiscent of the soft covering of an embryo.

**Figure 3.35**
Initial sketch of the design: the Organic House.

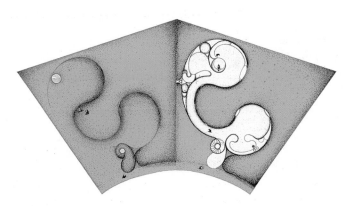

**Figure 3.36**
Drawing of the whole architectural Organic House, State of Mexico. Daniel Arredondo and Javier Senosiain, 1985.

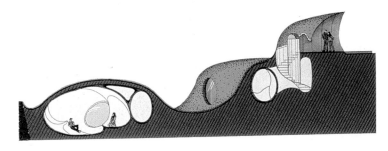

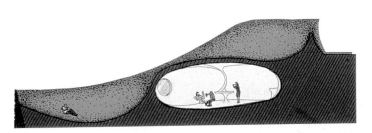

**Figure 3.37**
Architectural vertical sections. (a) Cross-section A-A´; (b) cross-section B-B´.

## Construction

In order to maintain fluidity in the structure, it was necessary to use a mouldable building material that could be shaped in a similar way to the modelling clay used for the models. It was also evident that since this was a house, the building material must not only possess the required plasticity but must also fulfil requirements that would make it more than a sculptural mass. After much investigation there was little doubt that ferroconcrete was the best solution. It promised a monolithic, resistant, mouldable structure of great elasticity.

The construction of the actual building began with a ferroconcrete frame which was placed over the outline, forming a metal skeleton in which the ribs were arranged like rings, varying in height according to the space required. The next step was to roll the ribs into the shape of a spiral.

With the framework assembled, two lengths of interwoven, enmeshed wire netting were attached, and concrete with little water content was cast on top. The concrete, cast or hurled like mortar, was transported through a flexible hose using air pressure and pneumatically sprayed with great force over the meshed wire surface. The blast of the jet was so strong that the impact of the material packed it solidly over the surface, increasing its resistance by 30 per cent. In this manner, a shell about 4 centimetres thick was achieved; it was resistant owing to its shape, impermeable, and easy to build. The top was afterwards covered with a 2 centimetre layer of sprayed polyurethane serving as waterproof insulation.

With the skeleton of the dwelling complete, the next step was to bury it. The idea was for the garden to cover the house, and fertile soil would be needed for that. Based on the principle of Japanese bonsai or dwarfed trees (the less deep the soil, the lower the trees grow), it was decided that the depth of the soil should fluctuate between 15 and 20 centimetres. This would ensure that the grass grew less tall and more slowly, resulting in lower gardening costs. The soil and grass would protect the membrane from sun, wind, hail and the yearly dry-rainy cycles, thus avoiding dilations that cause fissures and allow humidity to enter.

From the outside the house is nearly invisible – only grass, bushes, trees and flowers can be seen. To walk through the garden is to walk unknowingly over the roof of the house itself.

For the outline of the project's construction, a cross was marked in the middle of the terrain as a point of reference for the system of Cartesian coordinates, making it easier to pinpoint the centre of the circles. When free curves were involved, a garden hose was used in place of a curved metre. At this point, the outline of the house was traced and marked with stakes.

Later on, a little earth was removed from the centre of the outline, to be used in the formation of some small slopes. When those were finished, the whole thing looked rather like a skating rink: continuous and full of slaloms and raised ground.

**Figure 3.38**
Metallic frame
covered with wire
mesh.

**Figure 3.39**
Exterior view of the
Organic House.

## Microclimate

It's important to be able to control the climate in order to attain psychological and physical comfort. If a microclimate is to be created or maintained for the benefit of humans, it is best to begin with the outside and later continue with the private areas of the home.

The green barriers of trees and bushes, and the topography of the place, can be used to filter and prevent direct sunlight, creating shadows that protect the home from summer heat, dust and noise. They also refresh the atmosphere with evaporation and the transpiration of the foliage. When grass transpires, the absolute and relative humidity in the air increase close to the surface, producing conductive cooling. Meadows, trees and bushes are therefore preferable to any kind of paving, as they help maintain thermal balance in the atmosphere.

It's important to mention that the thermal characteristics of city surfaces are totally distinct from those in a purely natural environment – the penetration, reflection and absorption of light is different. In cities, the shapes of buildings, cars, pavements, and so on, create atmospheric refraction of heat, light and noise differently from that in the country.

Earth and sun work together in maintaining a stable temperature within the interior of the house, where the earth protects and the sun provides light and warmth. The windows of the house look out towards the most attractive views, preferably facing south for sunlight in winter, as winter-flowering plants do.

This kind of underground home is perhaps better lit and more sunny than a conventional home because its windows can be orientated in any direction, and the domes permit light and sunshine to enter from above. Ventilation is easy owing to the aerodynamic shape of the dwelling, which makes the free circulation of the air possible.

The internal temperature of the human body remains stable even though the external temperature varies; the same thing happens in buried homes. The soil acts as a stabiliser in changes of temperature, ensuring that cooling and warming effects above the earth do not immediately affect the house, at least not until diametrically different seasons are juxtaposed. This means that the soil around the house will be warmer in winter and cooler in summer. The house thus maintains constant temperatures of between 18 and 23°C all year long. The transpiration of grass, plants and trees adds refreshing coolness and oxygenates the atmosphere of the house, avoiding desiccation, infiltration of dust, and contamination.

During winter and summer alike, this microclimate conserves a relative average humidity of between 40 and 70 per cent, protecting inhabitants from respiratory illnesses and related complications.

## Inside the Dwelling

Access to the house is through a snail-like spiral entrance. There is a periscope so that whoever is in the kitchen can see who's ringing the bell. By the door there's a niche for visitors to leave their shoes, oriental style, and a stag-horn for umbrellas, overcoats and the like. The floor of the house is covered with a sand-coloured carpet, identifying the dwelling with the earth. This same colour covers the walls and the ceiling to achieve chromatic continuity.

The inside of the house is reached by descending through a tunnel to the living-room, to areas for eating and cooking, or to the furthest one, the sleeping area.

In the living-room, the curved window enlarges the visual perspective and has a projection on top to protect children in the garden, which also functions as an arch or structural beam and is comparable to eyelashes, which protect the eyes from sun, dust, wind and rain. The origin and essence of daily needs were analysed and, from the findings, furniture was fitted throughout the house. In the kitchen there are burners, a sink, and built-in shelves for the pantry; in the bedroom there are more cubbyholes for clothes, while in the bathroom, the taps of the basin, shower and bath have been replaced by waterfalls.

In the living-room the carpet is extended over a filling of small polyurethane balls, which takes on the shape of whoever is seated there. In ancient times, people were more rooted to the earth, in more contact and harmony with it – a relationship lost in urban environments. Even today, many cultures wash, cook, eat, rest and relieve themselves when squatting, kneeling or sitting, moulding knees and buttocks to the earth.

**Figure 3.40**
View of the tunnel.

**Figure 3.41**
View of the living-room from the tunnel.

There are also substantial savings in the foundations. Generally speaking foundations cost approximately 30 per cent of the total cost of conventional structures. The ferroconcrete shell distributes all stresses over the terrain, so that this foundation in itself is equivalent to the reinforced foundation of a conventional structure, with the advantage that it also has greater capacity for load transfer because of its shape and monolithic structure.

**Figure 3.42**
Aerial view of the Organic House.

**Figure 3.43**
The kitchen and living-room with a view to the garden.

**Figure 3.44**
View of the wash basin.

**Figure 3.45**
The bedroom and dressing-room.

## Shelter

*A free-form house that is buried is highly resistant to earthquakes. If we filled a shoebox with sand, placed a fresh egg in the middle, replaced the lid and shook the box violently, simulating the worst earthquake in history, the structure of the egg would remain intact (even though yolk and white may be mixed). A real earthquake would have a similar effect on the Organic House.*

If a tall, heavy tree fell on the underground house, it would hardly affect the structure, as the soil would absorb the shock of impact. The grass and soil protect this house from exterior fires; inside, the ferroconcrete structure is practically incombustible. Soil is also a magnificent acoustic insulation, reducing the noise of aeroplanes and automobiles.

## Troglodyte Economy

Finally, we come to some of the economic advantages of this type of construction; organic architecture may be a viable answer to the serious problem of housing shortage.

Comparatively speaking, structures made of ferroconcrete with a double curvature (shell) only need a third of the construction material used in a conventional house. The latter requires walls, floors and a roof that is some 15 centimetres thick, whereas ferroconcrete need only be 4 centimetres thick. The mortar also forms the finished base for paint, while (in the traditional system) bricks and stone have to be covered with the same mortar or plaster.

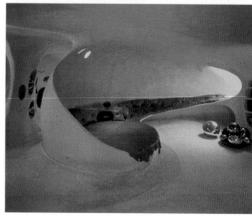

Further, wooden moulds for the concrete supporting posts are not necessary. It is easy to appreciate the value of this when remembering that the use of reinforced concrete shells was discontinued towards the end of the twentieth century, partly due to the high cost of the framework (construction materials and manual labour) that represented close to 50 per cent of the total cost of the building.

This kind of shape also increases the usable surface if it is equipped with the same perimeter as an orthogonal house. Using the circle and sphere as examples: these shapes contribute maximum space inside and minimum space outside, approximately 27 per cent of surface and volume, compared to the square and cube, respectively.

If we wanted a garden in a traditional house with the dimensions that a semi-buried building permits, we would need further land, with all the expenses that this brings – cost of land, title deeds and other documents, fences or walls, and the constant payment of land taxes.

The microclimate contributes to large savings in heating, and air conditioning in regions with extreme climates, a factor not always fully appreciated. In cities like Mexicali, southern California, for example, those who earn minimum salaries end up spending nearly half their income to maintain comfortable temperatures in their homes.

The most important thing, however, and a direct consequence of the advantages already mentioned, is that the user should feel better both physically and emotionally.

## The Shark: Evolving the Organic House

The Organic House was designed with just one bedroom, but as our family grew it became necessary to enlarge the accommodation. The extension was connected to the middle part of the original tunnel, from where two arms emerged, one ascending to the study close to the 'blue room' (television room), the other descending to the children's bedroom, which had a glass door to the garden protected by an overhang in the shape of a slide. To preserve privacy, the study was built on the upper level, giving a privileged view out to the National Park of Los Remedios. A terrace with a semi-covered Jacuzzi was added immediately below this extension. The function of these extensions and the views from the inside gave them the imaginary shape of a shark. This eminently free way of projecting organic spaces allows the shape to break with geometric rigidity and a right-angled way of thinking (Figures 3.47–3.50). Having your library-study inside a shark is something that perhaps Breton would have appreciated as it enables one to enjoy dreamy, structural movement which leads to architectural surrealism.

The monolithic structure is made of ferroconcrete. The semi-buried bedrooms act as foundations preventing the shark from turning over.

**Figure 3.46**
Access staircase to the study.

**Figure 3.47**
View from the study.

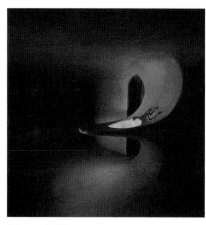

**Figure 3.48**
Wash basin.

**Figure 3.49**
Bedroom with bench.

**Figure 3.50**
Shark house exterior.

**Figure 3.51**
Proposal for a housing community in which public and private spaces are integrated.

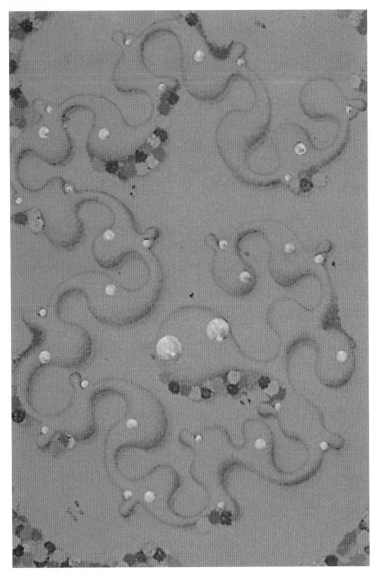

**Figure 3.52**
Detailed sketch of an organic community.

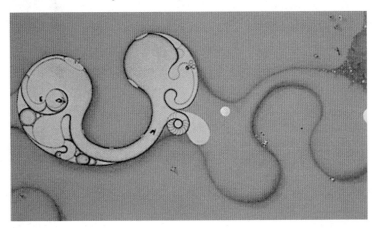

## A Whole Organic Community

Taking the Organic House as a starting point, designs for an organic community were drawn up. In these, problems of shared living were re-examined, aiming to improve the quality of the lives of its inhabitants and the concept in general.

Passages were created in the outside spaces using trees, bushes, and grass-covered slopes to separate green zones meant for common use from those meant for private use. Room was also created to give children and adults the opportunity to develop a liking for both family and neighbourly togetherness. A society modelled around natural elements permits one to see city planning not just as a set of streets to move along on, but also as an adventure based on fantasy scenes we imagined as children. It was proposed that electric carts for service and maintenance would be used inside this interconnected whole.

A series of grouped community services has been arranged for everyone to use: a laundry, ironing room, day-care centre, kindergarten, secretariat, meeting room, various shops and so on. A recreational zone has also been proposed with jungle gyms and other games for children, courts for different sports, and a cultural zone with a library, computer room, and exhibition gallery: all with the aim of reviving the nuclear concept of a close-knit neighbourhood. Use of underground ducts has been proposed for the infrastructure in order to manage the installations. Sufficient pipes with adequate capacity would be necessary to be able to register and modify them without having to disrupt anything for repair.

Of equal importance is the self-sufficiency of the community, for which proposed ecological techniques include a water treatment plant; family plots for gardening; production of fertilisers through the creation of compost heaps effectively using organic waste; utilisation of solar cells to harness available energy; heating of water by the sun; exploitation of aeolian energy; and so forth.

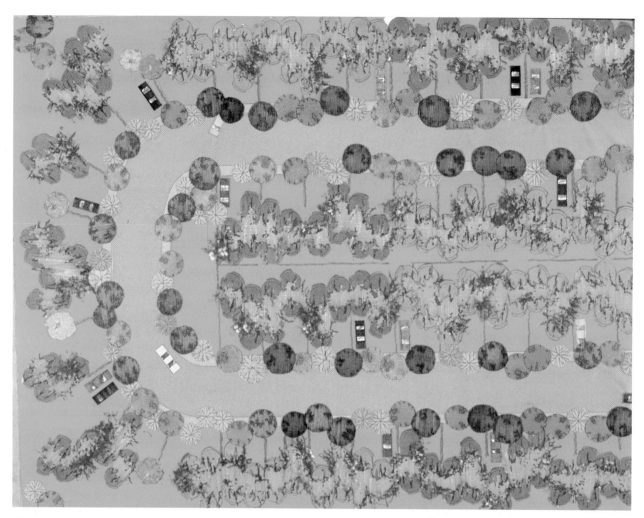

**Figure 3.53**
Illustration showing
an aerial view of
horizontal community
housing. Note the
irregular positioning
of the 'peanuts' so as
to avoid excessive
conformity.

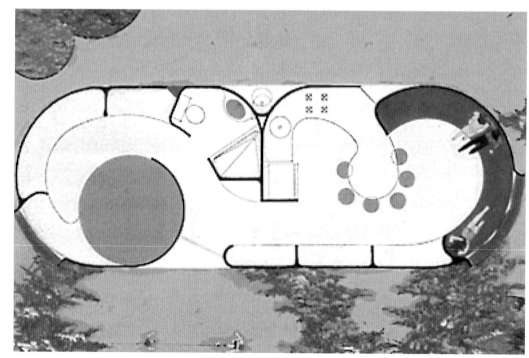

**Figure 3.54**
Architectural plan of
the 'peanut' module.
Alejandro Sánchez
de Tagle, Javier
Senosiain and Luis
Enríquez, 1989.

## Horizontal Community Housing

A housing project with terrain divided into lots of 7 metres wide and 20 metres deep was proposed. There is free space for cars to park in front of each lot. One or two modules in the shape of a peanut are situated on each lot, out of phase with each other to avoid excessive conformity in the community. The first 'peanut', for singles or couples, consists of three defined zones: *intimate*, with a double bedroom and storage area; *services*, with a bath and a kitchen, sharing a humid wall; *social*, with an area for food preparation spatially integrated with the living/dining room.

For future expansion, it would be possible to add another peanut in the middle, comprising two bedrooms with a multiple-use bathroom. One characteristic of this project is that, in spite of the small dimensions of each module (about 32 square metres), there is enough room to store clothing, food, books, electrical appliances, and so on, because almost the entire perimeter of the house is used for built-in furniture, leaving the central area free.

## System of Construction

Each peanut is made of ferroconcrete, in the prefabrication plant, with dimensions of 3.30 metres width by 10.50 metres length. These dimensions mean that the peanuts can be transported in trailer trucks and unloaded with a crane. Given that each module has integrated services available, the only connections that need to be made on site are water, electricity, and sewage pipes (drainage).

**Figure 3.55**
Architectural elevated
cross-sections.

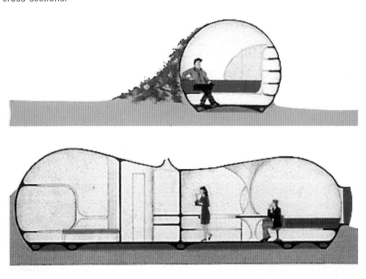

**Figure 3.56**
Prefabricated 'peanut' module which, due to its
dimensions, can be transported easily.

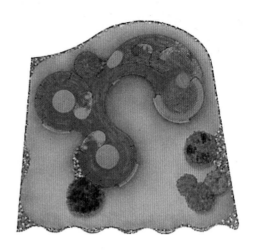

**Figure 3.57**
Architectural plans of
the Embryonic House,
Mexico. Daniel
Arredondo, Javier
Senosiain and Luis
Enríquez, 1992–1994.

**Figure 3.58**
Drawing showing
aerial view of the
access area to the
Embryonic House.

## The Embryonic House

The mass of the Embryonic House surrounds an
open space. The house is placed on a foundation
on uneven terrain, with a slope of about 3 metres
from the level of the street. The garage is located
at the same level as the street, from which a
spiral staircase takes one to the upper floor.

The essence of the concept is an organic
space incorporating formal, constructional
traditions inherent to the Mexican people; the
house is put together with polyurethane sprayed
over a pneumatic structure.

The constructional procedure is simple and
similar to that of papier mâché. The pneumatic
structure is anchored over a firm frame along the
whole length of the perimeter and then inflated
with a ventilator. Once the internal pressure is
correct, the polyurethane (liquid, plastic resins) is
sprayed on; when these resins are mixed and
make contact with the surface, the resultant

chemical reaction transforms them into a solid,
the volume of which is 30 times greater than
that of the liquid. Once this is finished, the
pneumatic balloon is deflated and can then be
reused.

A multicoloured covering of tiles is then
applied to the outside surface; these, from their
colour and weight, are reminiscent of some of the
Pre-Columbian pyramids. The stone talus
(footing) on the façade, a reminder of the
indigenous world, is used as a retaining wall, in
combination with cupolas made of over-baked red
brick.

Certain concepts, such as systems of
construction and constructional materials
introduced into Mexico during colonisation, are
repeated inside: the use of pavements of orange-
coloured clay briquettes in combination with
handmade tiles, for example. The walls and
ceiling are appropriately covered with stucco,
while the bathrooms are covered with a
collection of broken pieces of the same tiles
applied to the exterior surfaces forming irregular,
fanciful frets or borders in contrasting tones.

Spraying polyurethane over pneumatic
structures is like having a magic machine which
builds homes; our flexibility of imagination is the
only limitation to this. Here we have housing
that can be constructed as continuous areas
without joints or frame jambs between walls,
floor and ceiling, even including basic, built-in
furniture – beds, tables, wardrobes, bookcases
and cupboards – as part of the system. In this
way, the contemporary architect could find him
or herself in the enviable and inevitable role of a
nimble potter who creates dwellings.

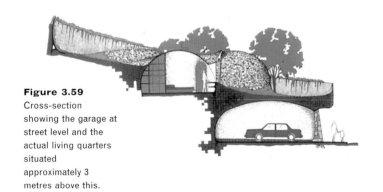

**Figure 3.59**
Cross-section
showing the garage at
street level and the
actual living quarters
situated
approximately 3
metres above this.

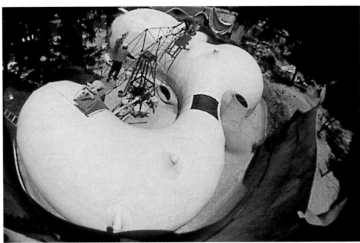

**Figure 3.60**
Photograph showing the process of spraying polyurethane over the pneumatic structure.

**Figure 3.61**
The façade of the Embryonic House. Sloped stone walls with inverted cupolas made of over-baked brick support the weight of the earth, while the summit made of ferroconcrete is covered with tiles and forged grillwork.

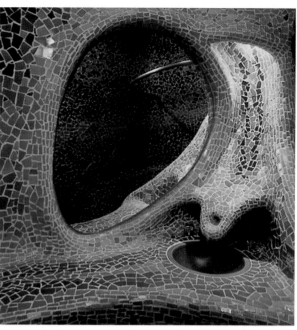

**Figure 3.62**
Exterior view of the Embryonic House. The dwelling encircles an open space. The mass, reminiscent of Pre-Columbian pyramids and sculptures, rises out of the earth like a whale at sea and forms grassy slopes that minimize the mass of the construction.

**Figure 3.63**
The bathroom covered with broken pieces of tile.

**Figure 3.64**
General view of the dining room and kitchen

**Figure 3.65**
Façade of the Flower House where the rainbow colours of the interwoven visor-like entrances with the retaining stone wall can be observed. Mexico. Javier Senosiain Aguilar and Luis R. Enriquez Montiel, 1993).

## The Flower House

The façade is an undulating stone wall that acts like a retaining wall. The vehicular and pedestrian accesses are framed with three visor-like crests made of ferroconcrete and covered with collected pieces of broken tile in softened colours of the rainbow.

The ascending access spiral at the entrance leads to the house itself, 3 metres above street level. The floor plan of the house resembles the shape of a flower with six petals, embracing a tile star in the corolla that surrounds a Jacuzzi in the centre, the exact mirrored image of the stained-glass star in the cupola.

Figure 3.66

**Figure 3.66**
Exterior view of the Flower House.

**Figure 3.67**
Flower house Jacuzzi and dining room.

**Figure 3.68**
View from the stained glass window. The star in the floor can be seen, while the one in the dome is reflected in the Jacuzzi.

**Figure 3.69**
Stained glass window.

Figure 3.67

Figure 3.68

Figure 3.69

**Figure 3.70**
Exterior view of the undulating façade.

The dwelling, with a surface area of 115 square metres, is based on the concept of the central patio, the perimeter rooms of the house converging on to it. It was achieved using the constructional system of pneumatic basis, with an overlying structural sandwich of mortar/sprayed polyurethane/mortar.

## The satellite Community

On a 30×30-metre lot located in Ciudad Satelite, a suburb of Mexico City, a small group of four houses was developed. The land, approximately 1.5 metres below street level, was used efficiently by partially burying the homes.

One's first impression comes from an undulating façade that resembles the form of two 'eagles.' Their wings spread, they envelop the four pedestrian entrances through which people enter. Each of the wings include a small storage room and access to the 'snail' entrance at garage level. This 'snail' entrance leads down to a multiple-use room, with a bathroom. The upper level area is also used for storing water and static butane gas tanks for each house.

On entering, the visitor crosses the multicoloured, undulating pavement of the garage with a view of the four cupolas of the houses, coloured in tones from yellow to red and framed by grassy dunes and Bougainvilleas which complement and merge with them.

Each house is independent of the others, in both services and access. The green areas, however, are integrated visually and spatially; the gardens of each house are delimited by bushes and footing walls.

The dwellings are based on a central patio and reflect Mexican traditions of construction in the finishes, colours and textures. The furniture and lighting are an intrinsic part of the architecture.

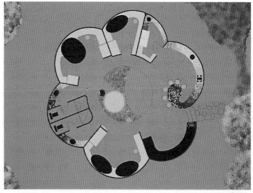

(a)

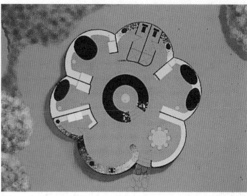

(b)

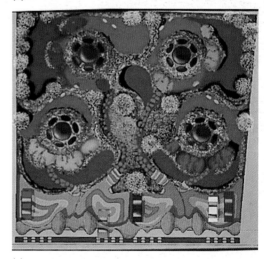

(c)

**Figure 3.71**
(a and b) Architectural floor-plan of the prototype of a house with an inside Jacuzzi and garden in the centre. Architectural floor-plan of the prototype of a house with the living-room in the centre space; (c) aerial plan of the group of houses. Javier Senosiain, Luis Enríquez. Mexico, 1995.

**Figure 3.72**

**Figure 3.73**

**Figure 3.74**

**Figure 3.72**
Panoramic exterior
view of the four
homes seen from the
main entrance.
**Figure 3.73**
Access to the
bathroom which has
multiple uses.
**Figure 3.74**
View of the dining-
room and kitchen.

.

The basic system of construction is a
pneumatic structure that forms the foundations
for everything else. Polyurethane is sprayed over
it and the balloon afterwards deflated. Exterior
and interior are both then smoothed with 5-
millimetre thick fibre cement. The result is a
structural 'sandwich', subsequently covered with
soil and grass.

# INDEX

(Page numbers in *italics* refer to figures)

Aalto, Alvar 115, *116*, 134
adobe *72*, 73–4, 78, 79, 140
aerodynamics 3–6, *132*
animals
    dwellings 18–24, 129–30
    skeletons 31, 37–8, 43, *44*, 105
    territory 17–18
    *see also* birds
arches 77–8, 82, 83–4, 118, *119*
architecture
    ancient Greek 53, 79
    ancient Roman 54, 80–1
    Baroque 54, 82, 87–8, 102
    Byzantine 54, 81–2, 91
    functional 9–12
    Gothic 7, 54, *83*, 84–5, 88, 135
    modern cities 93–6, 98–9, 100
    molluscs influencing *51*, 53–6, *57*, 58, 105
    nature's influence 28–44, 61, 66–76, 79
    organic 102–26, *127–8*, 134–5, 136, 139–58, 159
    rationalism 93, 103, 109
    Renaissance 54, 79, 82, 85, 87
    Romanesque 54, *82*, 83–4
    Romantic 54, 88, 105
    space 18, 92–3, 129–31, 135–7
    troglodyte 64, *65*, 66, 68, 139–45, *146*, 155–6
    vernacular 60–76, 110, 113, 114, 140
Arctic dwellings 70–1
art 14
    Baroque *86*, 87–8, 102
    Gothic *83*, 84–5
    painting 63–4, 74, *75*, 111, 114
    sculpture 54, 114, 124, 137
art nouveau 102–3
Atlántida church, Uruguay 117

Bachelard, Gaston 17, 56
Baroque architecture 54, 82, 87–8, 102
Barragán, Luis 10, *53*, 100
Bavinger House, Norman, Oklahoma *54*, 55
beaver lodges 23–4
bionics 3–8
birds 45, *46*, *132*
    eggs 37–8, 40
    nests 19–20
bricks 117, 118, *119*, 140, 150, *151*
bridges 27–8, *29*
Brunelleschi, Filippo 85, 87
Byzantine architecture 54, 81–2, 91

cable networks 32–5
Calatrava, Santiago *123*, 124–5
Candela, Felix 11–12, 28, 40–2, 44, 95
capitalism 95–6, 98

Cappadocia, Turkey 64, *65*, 66
Casa Batlló, Barcelona 106, *107*
Casa Milà, Barcelona *104*, 105–6
Castañeda Tamborrel, Enrique 116
cathedrals
    Brasilia 24, *25*, *26*
    Gothic *83*, 84, 135
    Renaissance 85, 87
    Romanesque *82*, 83–4
    St. John the Divine, New York *123*, 124–5
    *see also* churches
caves 15, *16*, 17, 62, 64, *65*, 66, 68
churches *10*, *40*, 118, *119*
    Atlántida, Uruguay 117
    Baroque 82, 87–8
    Notre Dame du Haut, Ronchamp, France 113–14, *115*, 135
    Renaissance 82, 85, 87
    Romanesque *82*, 83–4
    Sagrada Familia, Barcelona 108, 125
    St. Sophia, Istanbul 82, 87
    *see also* cathedrals
circulatory systems 30, *31*
cities
    architecture 93–6, 98–9, 100
    development 92–5
    organic 157
    origins 89–91
    planning 92–6, 99–100, 133
Ciudad Satelite, Mexico 155–6
climate
    influencing dwellings 70–6, 90–1, 125–6, *127*, *128*
    microclimates 142, 145, 158
Colani, Luigi 7
communities, organic 147, *148*, 149, 155–8
compression 29–30, 76
concrete 80, 102, 113, 116, 140, 141, 144–5, 149
construction techniques, animal 19–24
Cro-Magnon Man 63–4
curvature 39–42
curves 39–42, 131–3, 136–7, 141, 145, 150, *151–4*, 158
Cuvier, Georges 134

da Vinci, Leonardo *see* Leonardo da Vinci
dams, beaver 23, *24*
desert dwellings 72–5, 90–1
design
    process 11–12, *13*, 14, 140–1
    structural 27–30
Dieste, Eladio 117
Dogones people 72, 90–1
domes 34, 39–40, 78, 80–1, 82, 85, *86*, 87–8 *see also* vaults
Dulles Airport, Washington DC 34–5

dwellings
   animal 18–24, 129–30
   Arctic 70–1
   caves 17, 62, 64, 65, 66, 68
   cities 90–1, 92–3, 94, 95, 100
   climate influencing 70–6, 90–1, 125–6, 127, 128
   desert 72–5, 90–1
   earliest structures 68–9
   ecological 22, 125–6, 127, 128, 147
   jungle 75–6
   mobile 66–8
   organic 147, 148, 149–50, 151–2, 153, 154, 155–8
   Organic House, Mexico 139–45, 146
   social housing 116, 120
   space 135–7
   underground 64, 65, 66, 72, 131, 139–45, 146, 155–6
Dymaxion automobile 3–4, 5

ecological houses 22, 125–6, 127, 128, 147
eggs 37–8, 40
Egypt, ancient 79, 90
Embryonic House, Mexico 150, 151–2
Eskimos 70–1
evolution 2–3, 61–4
Expo'70, Osaka, Japan 33, 36–7

Faber, Colin 40, 41–2
Field of Miracles, Pisa, Italy 82, 84
flexion 29–30
flight 5–6
Flower House 153, 154, 155
Fuentes, Carlos 99
Fuji Pavilion, Osaka, Japan 36–7
Fuller, Buckminster 3–4, 5, 43–4
functionalism 9–12

Gaudí, Antoni 42, 103, 104, 105–8, 125, 135
geodesic structures 42–4
Goeritz, Mathias 10
Goff, Bruce 54, 55
Gothic architecture 7, 54, 83, 84–5, 88, 135
Greece, ancient 53, 79
Güell Park, Barcelona 106, 135
Guggenheim Museum of Art, New York 55, 57, 109

Hauser, Sanford 136
Hepworth, Barbara 137
houses see dwellings
humans
   nature influencing 2–3, 61–3
   space 16, 18, 92–3, 129–31, 135–7
   well-being 129–31, 135–7
Hundertwasser, Friedensreich 120, 157
Hungarian Pavilion, Seville 121, 122

igloos 70–1
Industrial Revolution 93, 95

Johnson Wax building, Racine, Wisconsin, USA 109, 110
jungle dwellings 75–6

Kenzo Tange 35, 55
Kiesler, Frederick 135, 136

Le Corbusier 9, 55, 113–14, 135
Le Duc, Viollet 84, 101, 105, 134
Leonardo da Vinci 5, 15, 17, 48, 49
López, Alfonso Olvera 59, 60

Maillart, Robert 27–8

Makovecz, Imre 121, 122
Manantiales restaurant, Xochimilco, Mexico 41
materials
   adobe 72, 73–4, 78, 79, 140
   bricks 117, 118, 119, 140, 150, 151
   concrete 80, 102, 113, 116, 140, 141, 144–5, 149
   plastics 32, 34, 37, 140, 141, 150, 156
   steel 32–5, 124, 141, 142
   tiles 150, 151–2
   timber 121, 122, 124
Mehl, Reine 130
Mendelsohn, Erich 113
Mesopotamia 78, 90, 91
microclimates 142, 145, 158
Mies van der Rohe, Ludwig 42
Mijares, Carlos 117, 118, 119
Miró, Joan 54, 103
mobile dwellings 66–8
molluscs 47, 48–56, 58, 105 see also shells
Moore, Henry 54, 137
Museo Eco, Mexico 10

nature
   and humans 2–3, 61–3
   influencing architecture 28–44, 61, 66–76, 79
   Nature Book 2, 3
   and science and technology 2–8, 19
   space 16–24, 129
   structures 25, 27–44
   see also climate; organic architecture
nautiluses 48, 50
Neanderthal Man 62, 63, 67
Neolithic Age 68–9
nests
   birds 19–20
   termites 21–2
Notre-Dame cathedral, Paris 83, 84
Notre Dame du Haut, Ronchamp, France 113–14, 115, 135
Nowicki, Matthew 32–3

Oasis 2000 Community 157
O'Gorman, Juan 111–13, 129, 134, 135
Opera House, Sydney 54, 55
organic architecture 102–26, 127–8, 134–5, 136, 139–58, 159
organic communities 147, 148, 149, 155–8
Organic House, Mexico 139–45, 146

painting 63–4, 74, 75, 111, 114
Palaeolithic Age 61–4
Palissy, Bernard 56
Pantheon, Rome 80–1
paths 132–3
patios 90–1, 155, 157
'peanut' modular houses 148, 149
pendentives 82
Picasso, Pablo 54, 107, 113
planning 92–6, 99–100, 133
plastics 32, 34, 37, 140, 141, 150, 156
pneumatic structures 35–7, 150, 156

Quetzalcoatl Canyon, Mexico 158

rationalism 93, 103, 109
Renaissance architecture 54, 79, 82, 85, 87
renewable energy 124, 125, 147
Rodin, Auguste 1, 11, 14
Romanesque architecture 54, 82, 83–4
Romanticism 54, 88, 105
Rome, ancient 54, 80–1

Saarinen, Eero 34–5, *38*, 42, *43*
saddle structures 32, 33, 40
Sagrada Familia, Barcelona 108, 125
Salmona, Rogelio 117–18
Santa Maria de la Fiore, Florence 85, 87
Santa María Tonantzintla, Puebla, Mexico *86*, 87–8
science, nature's influence 2–8, 19
sculpture 54, 114, 124, 137
shapes 45–6
    Antoni Gaudí 105
    curves 39–42, 131–3, 136–7, 141, 145, 150,
       *151–4*, 158
    designing 140–1
    molluscs *47*, 48–56, 58, 105
    snakes *13*, 158
    spirals 49–51, *53*, *54*, 55–6, *57*, 79, 143
shells 38–42, 48–50, *51*, *52*, 53–4, 55–6, 58
skeletons 31, 37–8, 43, *44*, 103, 105
social housing 116, 120
Solar Hemicycle house, Wisconsin, USA 110
solar power 124, 125, 147
space
    caves 15, *16*, 17, 62, 64
    human needs 16, 18, 92–3, 129–31, 135–7
spiders 32, *33*
spirals 49–51, *53*, *54*, 55–6, *57*, 79, 143
Sports Palace, Tokyo 35, *55*
squinches 82, 118
St. John the Divine cathedral, New York *123*, 124–5
St. Peter's Basilica, Rome 85, 87
St. Sophia church, Istanbul 82, 87
steel 32–5, 124, 141, *142*
stresses 29–30
structural principles 27–30
structures
    arches 77–8, 82, 83–4, 118, *119*
    cable networks 32–5
    domes 34, 39–40, 78, 80–1, 82, 85, *86*, 87–8
    earliest dwellings 68–9
    geodesic 42–4

igloos 70–1
lightweight 31–44
natural 25, 27–44
pneumatic 35–7, 150, 156
saddles 32, 33, 40
shells 38–42, 48–50, *51*, *52*, 53–4, 55–6, 58
vaults 37–42, 77, 78–9, 82, 83, 118
suburbs 93

technology, nature influencing 2–8, 19
tension 29–30 *see also* cable networks
tents 66–8
termite nests 21–2
territory 17–24 *see also* space
tiles 150, *151–2*
timber 121, *122*, 124
Tower of Babel 73, 78
trees 29, *31*, 120, *122*, 125, 140, 141
troglodyte architecture 64, *65*, 66, 68, 139–45, *146*,
    155–6
Tsui, Eugene 125–6, *127*, *128*
TWA terminal, Kennedy Airport, New York 42, *43*

underground dwellings 64, *65*, 66, 72, 131, 139–45,
    *146*, 155–6
University City, Mexico *13*, 112
Utzon, Jorn *54*, 55

vaults 37–42, 77, 78–9, 82, 83, 118 *see also* domes
vernacular architecture 60–76, 110, 113, 114, 140

well-being, human needs 129–31, 135–7
Wright, Frank Lloyd 14, 17
    cities 95, 100
    molluscs 55–6, 58
    organic architecture 109–10, 134

Yale University hockey rink 34

ziggurats 76, 78